## Praise for *Bark,*

"Lynn McKenzie takes you on a ⟨...⟩
enchanting that you might not ev⟨...⟩
erful skills as an animal intuitive as you simply follow her stories.

—Rebbie Straubing, DC, founder of the
Yoga of Alignment (YOFA®) and author of
*Rooted in the Infinite: The Yoga of Alignment*

"Enthralling real-life stories of people being enlightened by animals will inspire you to tap into your own intuitive communication and healing powers."

—Penelope Smith, animal communication specialist
and author of *Animal Talk, When Animals Speak,*
and *Animals in Spirit*

"A highly enjoyable and uplifting read … Full of humor, wisdom, and great love of animals and the healing bonds that endure beyond time."

—Vera Gabliani, PhD, clinical psychologist,
holistic practitioner, and trauma specialist

"Lynn McKenzie has written an enlightening book that reminds us of the higher spiritual purpose of our animal companions."

—Sunny Dawn Johnston, author of *Invoking the Archangels*
and founder of MySpiritualBiz.com

"*Bark, Neigh, Meow* not only encompasses powerful, real-life stories of unconditional love and clear communication between humans and their beloved animals, but also guides you on experiential journeys and simple exercises to make the connection for yourself."

—Lisa Aston Michael, animal Reiki master
and animal energy healer

"A heart-touching collection of deep and profound stories of animals as healers and soulful wisdom teachers ... Such a unique and creative approach to awakening the reader's intuitive and compassionate gifts for their animal companions."

—Regina Chante, LMT

"*Bark, Neigh, Meow* is a must-read for every animal lover. It demonstrates Lynn McKenzie's profound connection to the animals but more importantly leads the reader on a path to awaken the same connection within themselves."

—Julie Jeanne Bassett,
animal communicator and energy healer

"An essential read and positive teaching guide for anyone who cares for animals and wishes to communicate effectively with them."

—Leila Khoury, honors degree in occupational therapy
and with an MSc in emotional literacy and NLP

"Lynn McKenzie will bring tears to your eyes and joy to your heart with her amazing experiences and stories. The how and why are explained clearly so that you are able to actually do this with the exercises to practice and perfect your ability."

—Jeanette Saproni, MT (ASCP),
Reiki master, angel intuitive,
and canine massage educator

"*Bark, Neigh, Meow* is the perfect book that will guide you to direct communication with the special animal in your life."

—Donna Chicone, TEDx speaker and
award-winning author of *Being a Super Pet Parent*

"This book offers stories to help the reader understand how amazing communicating with animals can be, and further, each story, with its lesson, is followed by brilliant exercises to help us each individually achieve our goals."

—Barbara B. Welsch, DVM, PhD,
licensed veterinarian and psychologist

"*Bark, Neigh, Meow* will open your eyes to a spiritual connection with the animal kingdom … Every exercise provided was a step forward, and I found myself becoming more encouraged, and you will, too."

—Rochelle Perkins, MA, special needs educator

"I have been able to trust my inner instincts and trust what I have felt and heard knowing that Lynn's amazing knowledge and guidance are what have given me the courage and correct path to accomplish this."

—Lisa Needham, dog trainer

"A beautiful compilation of human/animal connections extraordinarily and vividly narrated for our enjoyment. The insightful lessons at the end of each chapter elevate our spirit and sense of knowing that animals are more than short-lived companions but rather spiritual teachers, healers, and guardians who transcend through time and many lives."

—Adriana Seidl, DVM, CEO of Gypsy Dog & Doc Inc.
and founder of the Creature Covenant movement

# bark,
# neigh,
# meow

## About the Author

Lynn McKenzie (Cottonwood, AZ) is an expert in the animal intuitive and energetic fields with over thirty years of experience. She has coached and consulted with over one hundred thousand clients, and she offers programs relating to animal communication, healing, spiritual growth and personal transformation, psychic development, clairvoyance, and chakra healing.

*Awaken to the Transformative Wisdom
of Your Companion Animal to
Activate Your Soul's Highest Calling*

# bark,
# neigh,
# meow

## Lynn McKenzie

Llewellyn Publications
Woodbury, Minnesota

FIRST EDITION
Second Printing, 2023

Cover design by Shannon McKuhen
Chakra figure on page 50 © Mary Ann Zapalac
Interior art on pages 35, 103, 130, 145, and 264 by Angela Wix, all other art by the Llewellyn Art Department.

Llewellyn Publications is a registered trademark of Llewellyn Worldwide Ltd.

**Library of Congress Cataloging-in-Publication Data**
Names: McKenzie, Lynn, author.
Title: Bark, neigh, meow : awaken to the transformative wisdom of your companion animal to activate your soul's highest calling / Lynn McKenzie.
Description: First edition. | Woodbury, Minnesota : Llewellyn Worldwide, Ltd, [2021] | Includes bibliographical references.
Identifiers: LCCN 2020057239 (print) | LCCN 2020057240 (ebook) | ISBN 9780738765945 (paperback) | ISBN 9780738766225 (ebook)
Subjects: LCSH: Pets—Anecdotes. | Human-animal relationships—Anecdotes.
Classification: LCC SF416 .M35 2021  (print) | LCC SF416  (ebook) | DDC 636.088/7—dc23
LC record available at https://lccn.loc.gov/2020057239
LC ebook record available at https://lccn.loc.gov/2020057240

Llewellyn Worldwide Ltd. does not participate in, endorse, or have any authority or responsibility concerning private business transactions between our authors and the public.

All mail addressed to the author is forwarded but the publisher cannot, unless specifically instructed by the author, give out an address or phone number.

Any internet references contained in this work are current at publication time, but the publisher cannot guarantee that a specific location will continue to be maintained. Please refer to the publisher's website for links to authors' websites and other sources.

Llewellyn Publications
A Division of Llewellyn Worldwide Ltd.
2143 Wooddale Drive
Woodbury, MN 55125-2989
www.llewellyn.com

Printed in the United States of America

## Disclaimer

Animal communication and healing is not a substitute for veterinary or medical care. Please consult a veterinarian, medical doctor, or psychiatrist for any and all health concerns. If you or someone you know is struggling with suicidal ideation, please reach out to a mental health expert. If you are within the US, you may use this hotline:

National Suicide Prevention Lifeline
1-800-273-8255

# Dedication

*To all my teachers, human and animal,
with love and gratitude.*

# Acknowledgments

I'd like to thank my family for their unwavering love and support, in life and in this project—especially my mom, Helen Madsen, for the countless hours spent listening to or reading various incarnations of this book … at age ninety, no less!

I thank each of my friends for their support, enthusiasm, and understanding as I sequestered myself away during the creative process of planning, writing, and editing this book, unavailable for much else. If you are one of the ones who spent time listening to or reading chapters for me, you'll never know how much that helped. I'd especially like to thank Linda Pizzale for the many phone conversations spent poring over the details of my book, listening to my ideas, leading me to deeper clarity, offering suggestions, and giving me honest feedback at every juncture. You are a gem and went way above and beyond the call of duty for a friend!

A special thanks to Tamara Beach, Melinda Folse, and Sam Horn, without whom this book wouldn't have been born.

I would like to honor and express gratitude for my clients and students who have been inspiring me daily since 1993, especially those who allowed me to share their stories here. Even if your story wasn't chosen for this book, you are a blessing and a source of inspiration, grace, and unending gratitude in my life.

A special thanks to my literary agent, Sharon Bowers, and my publisher, Llewellyn Worldwide, and my main contact there, Acquisitions Editor Angela Wix.

And to the animals: you are everything!

# Contents

*List of Exercises*   *xvii*

*Introduction: Animals Are Far More*
  *Than Just Companions*   *1*

## Section One: Animal Companion as Partner
**Chapter 1:** Finding a Soul Connection   13
**Chapter 2:** Experiencing a Deep Bond   25
**Chapter 3:** A Divine Appointment   39

## Section Two: Animal Companion as Teacher
**Chapter 4:** Seeing Things in a New Way   57
**Chapter 5:** Learning About Life and Leadership   71
**Chapter 6:** Opening to Intuition   83

## Section Three: Animal Companion as Guide
**Chapter 7:** Receiving Transformational Breakthroughs   97
**Chapter 8:** An Unconventional Guide   109
**Chapter 9:** Letting Go   121

## Section Four: Animal Companion as Healer
**Chapter 10:** Healers in Fur   137
**Chapter 11:** A Glimmer of Hope   151
**Chapter 12:** Daring to Be Vulnerable   165

## Section Five: Animal Companion as Catalyst
**Chapter 13:** Feeling Connected   179
**Chapter 14:** Nudged Toward Destiny   191
**Chapter 15:** Achieving Dreams with Direction   205

**Section Six: Animal Companion as Bridge**

**Chapter 16:** Receiving Comfort from Beyond    219
**Chapter 17:** Overcoming Despair    231
**Chapter 18:** A Conduit for Healing    245
**Chapter 19:** A Winged Ambassador    257

*Conclusion: Activate Your Soul's Highest Calling*    269
*Recommended Resources*    273
*Bibliography*    275

# Exercises

Opening the Connection   21

Linking Energy Fields   34

Deepening Your Connection   49

Tuning In   67

Meeting Your Guides and Helpers   79

Discovering Your Spirit Animal   91

Opening to Guidance   106

Balancing Your Chakras   117

Reading Their Chakras   129

Receiving Healing from the Animals   145

Opening Your Channels   160

Creating Inner Peace and Trust   175

Sending and Receiving Messages   187

Interpreting Their Messages   200

Opening to Their Inspiration   213

Signs from Animals in Spirit   228

Communicating with Animals in Spirit   240

The Gift of Your Animal Companion   253

Healing Portals Sent from Spirit   263

Introduction

# Animals Are Far More Than Just Companions

*Some people talk to animals.*
*Not many listen though. That's the problem.*

~A. A. MILNE

Have you ever looked at your animal companion and wondered what they may be trying to tell you?

Undoubtedly, you know when they are hungry, tired, or sick. You probably know when your animal friend is happy, sad, or angry. You may even feel close enough to tell when they have a specific need or even a want. But have you paid closer attention … have you really *listened*? Have you ever thought that the way we communicate with animals could go deeper—much deeper—than simply the basics? What if animals could converse with you, guide you in your life, give you advice, help you heal, or even be the catalyst to opening your life up to a path entirely different from the one you know?

It is my firm belief that animals were put on this earth not only to be friends and companions for us, but to share their deep, divine wisdom with us; each animal possesses this wisdom and eagerly wants to impart it to us. It's also my belief that all sentient beings are equal and that animals have souls and a spiritual essence just as humans do. No animal is here by accident; each one has a unique purpose to fulfill. What if an animal's express purpose in life was to partner with, guide, and teach *you*?

Think back to any of the animal friends you've shared your life with. What drew you to them? Now, think about it from their perspective. What do you think drew them to you? Most of us look for a meaningful connection with an animal—and they can absolutely make their preferences very clear to us. You may have had an animal companion that you instantly connected with or one you felt was your soul mate. This feeling isn't imagined or created by you; it is organized by the universe to bring you and your animal friend together for any number of divinely orchestrated reasons that will be carried out during your time together. Animals, I believe, are an untapped resource that can bring so much more meaning into our lives as vehicles of healing, learning, and connection to our soul's purpose.

In addition, it has been my experience—and many others can attest to this—that while we often may feel like we have chosen, saved, or rescued our pets, it may indeed be the other way around. Animals help us through tough times and are amazingly resilient and resourceful. There is much healing comfort to receive from them when we pause and accept it. In appreciation for our love, partnership, and care, their love for us returns tenfold.

For these reasons and so many more, I'd like to invite you to consider the idea that animals are much more than they seem—and they offer so much more than we often give them credit for. Truly, animals can change our lives—in more ways than we can imagine—if we are open to allowing them to do so. I believe that by increasing our understanding of the ways other species communicate with us, particularly those domesticated animals with whom we have developed the deepest relationships, we can continue to create wonderful, life-changing experiences with them that we may have missed out on had we not paid attention. Animals have the power and ability to transform any area of our lives into our ultimate destiny, helping us fulfill our dreams and reach our true potential, where we feel most fulfilled and at peace.

If you're wondering how to realize the full transformational power and wisdom of animals, you have picked up the right book. Even if you do not currently have an animal companion, you most likely have had one in the past, or maybe you know someone with one that you're very fond of. These animals—and the animals all around us—are there to help, heal, and commune with us if we will but stop and listen. It may be as simple as a bird chirping near your window or a squirrel scurrying from tree to tree, a butterfly fluttering across your path, or a stray or neighborhood dog or cat stopping by to say hello. Once you are fully aware of the life that animals can breathe into your own, you may never be able to look at nature the same way again.

We often get so immersed in our busy, hectic lives that we neglect slowing down and appreciating nature, much less the animals all around us and the companion animals that share our daily lives. The first step if you want to hear from your animal friend? Slow down, quiet your mind, and pay attention. Everything in nature is a divinely inspired gift to be appreciated, and animals are certainly no exception. Every animal has its own divine wisdom to share with us if we're open to it.

Having emerged from the womb loving animals, I have always felt at home with them and in tune with their nature. From the time I was a child, I was going out of my way to be around animals, to take care of them, and to commune with them. When I was as young as two years old, my parents began to notice how drawn I was to animals. They tell me I spotted a big German shepherd one day, and I ran right up to him just like he was an old friend. My mother—a first-time parent who was pregnant with my sister at the time—panicked, not knowing how the large dog would react. She later admitted she was terrified and felt powerless to stop me, as she couldn't seem to catch me before my little legs sped off toward the dog. Thankfully, he was a very sweet and gentle soul who allowed my childlike attention and likely enjoyed returning the love.

When I was on a family road trip a few years later, I happened to see a rabbit on the road who had been the unfortunate victim of a passing car. Apparently, I was deeply affected by seeing this deceased animal and asked numerous questions: Who was this bunny? Why had this happened to him? Where was his mom? What about his brothers and sisters? Where was he now? My adult self wonders just how much I knew as a child of the concept of the soul, and I think I may have had an inherent idea that the bunny's soul was alive and well elsewhere even at that young age. Either way, I think my parents were incredibly glad when we reached our destination, because I asked them questions during the entire drive. However, the questions kept coming for weeks afterward!

Of course, I had no conscious idea when I was a child or even a young adult that each of my experiences with an animal and the deep connections I formed would lead me to what would ultimately be revealed to me as my life's calling and deepest passion—being an animal intuitive, healer, and teacher who now guides others toward discovering their unique gifts and abilities with the help of their animals. All I knew was that I loved animals, felt comfortable around them, and even felt like I *needed* to be around them. It was truly second nature for me and a foreign concept that anyone would *not* feel that way.

As it turned out for me, it took the nudging and guidance of a few animals in my own life to get me to the path that led me to where I am today. Once I reached the point where I was able to hear and accept the guidance and advice of my cherished animal friends, I not only found my destiny, but also discovered profound fulfillment in my soul. It wasn't somewhere I ever planned or expected to be—but it turned out to be exactly where I was meant to be.

Beforehand, I had a successful real estate career and was reasonably happy. I could have continued on that path, but I felt that something was missing. I knew deep down that real estate wasn't my calling, but at the time, I wasn't sure exactly what my true calling was. Then, I discovered the field of animal communication, a vocation I hadn't even been aware of, and as I studied it, I was able to see my path clearly. It was irresistible, and I soon felt more peace, joy, and fulfillment than I'd ever imagined I could feel.

It wasn't as if I jumped right into animal communication, either; it was somewhat of a gradual process. While still working in real estate, I began studying to be a spiritual psychotherapist, and elements of that training ignited a fire within me to learn as much as possible as I could about metaphysics. I spent the next fifteen years studying every intuitive, energetic, and healing training I could find, learning everything I could about the invisible realm. As I learned and grew, it was my intent to work with people, so the animal aspect of my work took me by surprise. Once I discovered the possibility of using what I had learned with animals, it all fell into place, and I was able to combine everything as the destination revealed itself to me. Looking back now after twenty-seven years in this field, I can see how all that had transpired in my life led me to this point—the culmination of my passion and purpose. The signs were there all along; I only had to discover my purpose for myself and take that step toward it!

I tell you this about myself so you can see that my calling and current abilities took time to manifest; they weren't evident to me from the start. Each of us has the ability to find our own path of awakening in our own time and in our own way; I'm simply here to tell you that you, too, can find yours, and animals exist to help you do exactly that. If you feel unfulfilled in your current career or situation, I want you to know that it doesn't have to stay that way. Your dreams can come to fruition; your life can be fulfilling. We all have divine gifts that the universe wants us to share with the world, but first, we have to recognize and accept them for ourselves.

I created the title "animal intuitive" back in the early 1990s as a way to refer to my work to set it apart, since most in my field use "animal communicator" as their title. The difference is mainly that an animal communicator receives their information directly from an animal—through feelings or perception at or over a distance. This is also known as interspecies telepathic communication. The information I receive comes to me, however, through a variety of different channels: telepathy—the same way animal communicators receive, but also through my psychic/intuitive gifts—from my guides, angels, the universe, source energy, and so on; clairsentience, or empathic feeling; and claircognizance, or clear knowing without knowing exactly how you know. Each of these paths or methods are equally important and useful when helping the animals.

I also have a huge passion for healing, having studied it for decades, and I feel the term *animal intuitive* nicely highlights the healing work I do.

I realize that some of the concepts mentioned in this book may be a bit of a stretch for you as the reader. Perhaps you love animals but don't feel like an overly spiritual person, or maybe you picked the book up because you were drawn to the cover. No matter the reason, you're here now, reading, and this fact alone is not without purpose. Divine timing has brought you here, and I encourage you to keep an open mind in regard to what you may experience. If you do, I can promise you won't close this book without feeling some type of transformation in your heart and your soul. No matter your age, education, background, or achievements, everyone can benefit from expanding their consciousness. Growth is what keeps us vibrant and alive; otherwise, we remain stagnant. There is always so much more in life to learn and discover.

Regardless of the number of years I have been doing this work with people and animals, and no matter how many experiences I've had, I never cease to be amazed at the truths and awareness I am opened up to on a regular basis. Each experience offers unique opportunities and new concepts to discover—the parts that make up the whole that is our journey on this earth. Approach this book with an open mind and a willing spirit; if you tap into the timeless wisdom and use the suggestions I've compiled in this book, your life will be better for it.

If you are already familiar with some of the concepts presented in this book, that is wonderful as well. This will simply be a deeper dive into what you already know and have experienced, and it will allow you to see the perspectives of others. Regardless of your level of expertise with animals and your prior spiritual encounters, I am positive you will read something in this book that will affect you, resonate with you, and touch you on some level—most likely, multiple levels.

This book is divided into six sections that encompass all that animals are and can be for us—partners, teachers, guides, healers, catalysts, and bridges. Each section will explore the ways that animals share these roles with us and will provide practical, relatable examples. There are three chapters to every section except the last one, which has four. Each chapter tells a story about a specific animal or two. A few stories are my own, and the rest are stories told to me by clients I have worked with over the years. All the stories are true, although some of the names and details have been changed for privacy and confidentiality purposes. Regardless, each story has its own impact and meaning, some of which will resonate deeply with you. Keep in mind as you read over the stories that each one can apply to any animal, regardless of species, so simply because a story is about a horse, that doesn't mean that one line of communication, healing, or transformation applies to only a horse. You might find that you relate to or receive information from certain animals better than others, and that's normal; however, you can think of goats, iguanas, chickens, or llamas as companion animals, too, not just the standard dogs, cats, and horses.

If you're feeling a bit skeptical, I'd like to challenge you to select and read just *one* of the stories to see if you're not touched in some way. Remember, all these stories have been someone's real-life experiences.

At the end of each chapter, you will find a lesson and then a reflection section that will help you apply the theme of the story to your own life while contemplating relationships and experiences with the animals you have known or encountered. After each reflection, you will find an exercise you can do to become more connected with the animals in your life and also to begin communicating with them to receive their divine wisdom. I'll give you simple steps that will gradually but steadily lead you toward discovering some of the most profound insights you'll ever experience—even from the beloved animal friend or friends right next to you. They are all eagerly waiting for you to hear what they have been wanting to tell you!

All the exercises are designed to lead you toward your own experiences in your own way, and each one builds upon the last, taking you deeper with each chapter. I encourage you in advance to read them slowly and ponder them, and then circle back and revisit them after you've read the entire book. You'll most likely find that you get more out of each exercise after you've finished the book, and all your experiences will come together more clearly. The more you practice each exercise, the more benefit you will receive.

Our animal companions enrich our lives in many positive ways. They come into our lives to make a difference in the way we live, in our relationships with others, and in the way we fulfill our life's true purpose. Once you begin seeing animals differently— the way they wish to be seen, as beings designed to enlighten and empower us—all your experiences with them will begin to change. Simply opening your mind up to all that animals have to offer can be the catalyst to giving and receiving deeper fulfillment and relationships with them as well as others around you.

In closing, I'd like to leave you with a quote from Abraham Maslow, psychologist, lifelong student of human behavior, and creator of the well-known Maslow's Hierarchy of Needs: "In any given moment we have two options: to step forward into growth or to step back into safety."[1] Remaining in safety may be the most comfortable, but stepping forward is what opens your mind, your heart, and your soul to new experiences that can change your life and bring you infinite rewards.

So take the plunge with me; see what you can learn from my experiences as well as those of others. Discover the transformations you can undergo and the deeper meanings you can uncover in your own life and in the lives of your animal companions. I strongly believe you will be glad you did.

---

1. Abraham H. Maslow, *The Psychology of Science: A Reconnaissance* (New York: Harper & Row, 1966), 22.

# section one
# Animal Companion as Partner

# Chapter 1
# Finding a Soul Connection

*My treasure does not glitter in a jeweled box;*
*she gleams in the sun and neighs in the night.*
~BEDOUIN PROVERB

I like old sayings like the Arab proverb above. They remind us that life should be poetic rather than brash. As any horse person will attest, neighing in the night is a wonderfully mystical sound, a piece of heaven on earth. Before I discovered my calling working with people and animals, I lived and worked in the practical business world for more than twenty-five years, selling real estate in my native Canada. Unbeknownst to me, throughout those years—and indeed, my whole life—I was being groomed by many different animal friends to write about my first true connection: Jasmine, a beautiful horse who was wild at heart and had a mind of her own.

Jasmine's story begins well before we met, as does my own. I grew up in Toronto at a time when the city was still surrounded by tracts of undeveloped countryside, with clusters of woods and open farmland within easy reach; as soon as I was old enough, I would escape there at every opportunity.

Around the age of thirteen, my friend Judy and I were out one day, riding our bikes, enjoying the fresh air and open roads. The road led us past a horse farm. Split rail fences lined the property, and several horses grazed in the cool grass. "That's what we should do," announced Judy as we pulled our bikes over and gazed at the horses. "Get a job working on a horse farm."

"No one would pay us," I told her. "We know nothing about horses."

"Who cares if they pay us?" Judy grinned.

As I gazed at the horses grazing peacefully, I realized she was right. Just being out there would be reward enough.

I soon landed a job at a local horse farm, exchanging my work for the chance to ride the horses. I cleaned stalls, fed and looked after horses, and rode every chance I could get. I liked all the horses, but I fell in love with a beautiful big black mare called Midnight. Midnight was 17.2 hands high (meaning her back was 5'8", a good 3½" taller than me) and had a sweet temperament; I rode her almost every day. When she went up for sale, I begged my parents to buy her, but they did not think my plan for horse ownership was either sensible or affordable.

I was devastated when Midnight left, but her departure only hardened my resolve. Although I was only fourteen, I landed a paying job and saved every penny I earned. I was determined to buy a horse. My parents were still against the notion, and whenever I raised the idea, I was told, "You are not going to buy a horse, Lynn; that's all there is to it."

But I was as stubborn and independent as the horses I cared for, and I would not take no for an answer. As a horse-crazed teenager, it felt like life or death to me—I had to have a horse to love, care for, and learn from just as much as I needed air to breathe. In a few short months, I went from not even thinking about horses to "girl gone horse-crazy."

I guess my diligence and hard work paid off, for as my fifteenth birthday approached, my parents announced that I would finally be allowed to purchase a horse. To get me started, they were going to buy me a saddle for my birthday. This was a big deal—saddles can cost more than some horses, especially the ones I could afford, so I knew how lucky I was. The saddle they bought me was a high-quality English-style jumping saddle made in Germany, which actually did cost more than my first horse.

With their approval, my spirits soared, stoking my impatient teenage nature. I was about as typical a teen as you can get, with a great group of friends and a boyfriend on the football team, but all of that paled for me beside the prospect of owning a horse. I would lie on my bed visualizing myself caring for and riding my own horse, both in the ring and out in the forest, and every day I would circle the horse ads in the *Toronto Star* classifieds, terrified that my parents would change their minds before I found "the one."

Finally, the day came. My father took me to see one of the horses I'd seen in an ad: a bay mare. At that point, I would have bought just about any horse, but when we got there, we discovered that she had a flaw: she was a "weaver." Weavers repetitively move their head and neck from side to side while shifting their weight back and forth, a genuine "stable vice."

I would have overlooked almost any fault, probably even the lack of a limb. But as my riding instructor pointed out, the horse I had fallen in love with would suffer excessive physical wear and tear in her joints from this vice, causing a lifetime of problems. Furthermore, many stables would not welcome her as a boarder, because weaving, which develops as a result of excessive confinement in a stable, can be contagious. A horse's "natural" habitat is where they roam wild, not penned up in a stable—or a truck.

I mention a truck because, at my father's urging to find us a better horse, the stable owner called a local horse dealer, who showed up one day in a sixteen-foot stake-bed truck jammed full of a half dozen horses, all packed together like sardines in a can. The first horse off the truck was a sooty buckskin mare with a black tail that nearly reached the ground and a disheveled dark mane. She appeared keenly aware of her predicament and looked to be on high alert, and I instantly fell in love with her.

Her slightly disreputable appearance and twitchy demeanor matched that of the dealer, a rakish fellow with a rolled-up cigarette hanging from his bottom lip who seemed more interested in dumping horses on innocent teenagers than whether they had ever been trained or ridden, but to my teenage self, she was beautiful, sleek, and gleaming, like a Maserati sports car. In reality, she was somewhat scruffy, still wearing her winter coat with a sloppy hunter clip, probably done at the last minute to make her look the part of an English riding horse. She was definitely a diamond in the rough, and I was probably the only one who could see it. Despite her faults, it felt as though fate had meant for us to find each other.

I named her Jasmine, and when I got my feet back on the ground, I could see that I had light-years of work cut out for me. I rode her immediately. She felt free under my seat, and despite her scruffy appearance, I instinctively knew that Jasmine was beautiful inside. But she had come to help educate me in the nuances of the spiritual world, as well as the physical, emotional, and mental worlds, too; immediately, she put me to her test. Without warning, she reared up on her hind legs, almost tipping over backward. I stuck with her, and as she rose up, I loosened the reins, leaned forward, and held on tight to her neck, one of the maneuvers my trainer had taught me. Jasmine was not done with me yet, however, displaying her acrobatic skills with the best leap, twist, and buck I've ever experienced, a rodeo-worthy performance. Again, despite her best efforts, she couldn't unseat me, and in resisting her continuing efforts, I soon acquired a seat so strong that no future mount ever had a chance of dumping me. I had passed my test.

The two of us eventually became one. Not so much physically, although that closeness probably saved my neck a time or two, but in a spiritual bond that has not left me to this very day. I didn't realize it at the time, of course, but through my time with Jasmine, I was rapidly absorbing otherworldly insights on a soul level, unknowingly being prepared to connect deeply with all animals.

I quickly learned that the time I spent with Jasmine felt more profound to me than any other relationship I had in my busy teenage life. I felt compelled to spend every possible moment with her. Every afternoon I'd dash home from school, make myself a quick snack—usually just a peanut butter sandwich—then jump on the northbound Markham Transit bus to the horse farm. Most days, I would ride Jasmine, but even if I wasn't actually riding her that day, I would care for her, curry her coat, and talk with her constantly. All day at school, I had thoughts about what I'd discuss with her, and I'd stay in the barn until dark, when my parents would come to pick me up.

Our relationship soon became a deep soul connection. We spent so much time together that we became one in spirit, with Jasmine helping to connect me with nature and all the other aspects of my life on a whole new level. Even my friends could see it.

I knew I was horse-crazy, but little could I have predicted that this horse and I would have such a deep and magical connection, becoming so much more than best friends. Of course, we both continued with our own individual habits: Jasmine would rear, leap, buck, and twist, and I would hang on tenaciously, a grin of pure happiness plastered on my face.

In time, I moved her to a more upscale horse farm where we could ride through acres of wooded trails and experience the true magic of nature together. I taught her to jump in the arena, and we soon graduated to riding cross-country through open farmland and even in the woods, often bareback. Was it dangerous? Probably, but when we were out together, we didn't fear anything.

Despite our closeness, Jasmine maintained her independence and always made her boundaries clear. If she didn't want to jump, she wasn't going to, no matter what! Her coat changed shades with the seasons, like autumn leaves, but in spirit, she never left the wild, remaining faithful to her true self. Indeed, out in the wilder open spaces where we now roamed, she taught me to sense the instinctive world that came naturally to her and, eventually, to me. Jasmine possessed a herd instinct and seemed to communicate easily with me, as she might have communicated with other horses. She never ran away from me, always with me, though often in the direction of her choosing.

Horses are not particularly vocal animals, with just four basic vocalizations: the neigh or whinny, the nicker, the squeal, and the snort. They also make sighing, grunting, or groaning noises at times. Jasmine used all these sounds, and she also communicated through body language: the position of the ears and the neck, nuances of posture, and probably ways yet to be discovered by humans.

When I rode Jasmine in the woods and across open spaces, I could *feel* her exhilaration in being closer to the wild. I felt it in her step, through my seat, and in every fiber of my being. The instincts she felt, I felt. We blended our energies, and I would later look back on that combined synergy as the beginning of the opening of my psychic gifts, something that I eventually learned to impart to others—a faith in a broader sensing of what life is all about, the way animals feel it.

Occasionally, when we ran free in the woods, Jasmine would look up or to the side suddenly, as though she'd heard something. By about the fourth time this happened, I was finally able to spot what had attracted her attention: a gorgeous red-tailed hawk, soaring high above us. It wasn't until later that I truly began to understand the connection and significance behind her notice of them.

Jasmine became my jeweled treasure, gleaming in the sun and neighing in the night. Over time, our relationship went from a place of "wild" to being able to ride her not just out on the trails, but also on the road. She even allowed me to train her enough to attend shows. But it was our time together out in nature that developed the magic, our time breathing the free air that helped us become one in spirit. I had always felt sensitive to animals— dogs, cats, you name it—but now, I had begun to grow and transform, to strengthen that connection thanks to Jasmine.

From Jasmine's time forward, I began to sense and feel what animals knew and wanted to communicate to humans. This perception is mystical, but at the same time has a long and well-documented history, with a Greek physician first writing about the connection to horses as long ago as 460 BCE. Today, psychologists employ the knowingness and sensitivity of horses for experiential learning, healing, psychotherapy, and education, for both personal transformation and corporate team-building. My time with Jasmine enabled me to develop a much broader psychic perception, which is made up of equal parts sensory perception and something mystical from the invisible realm where animals share thoughts and feelings. That's one of the things this book is about, and I shall forever be grateful to Jasmine, my first horse, my first love, for what she taught me.

## Lesson

Animals connect deeply with us, but it can take us time to realize it on a conscious level. Often, it's only in hindsight that we recognize the depth of the partnership and the far-reaching threads of the bond we share. The more time we spend with the animals, the easier it becomes to recognize the magnitude of the kinship we experience, and the more we benefit from our connection.

For me, it was Jasmine who initiated my connection to nature and to the invisible realm. My partnership and bond with her established the foundation for recognizing my own psychic and intuitive nature, and through osmosis, she taught me to sense the instinctive world that came so naturally to her.

Horses are wonderful beings to initiate us into deep partnership. When you're sitting on a horse, your entire body is immersed in the brilliance and magic of their energy field. For my partnership with Jasmine to flourish, not only did I have to surrender control and let go of myself and my own agenda, I had to trust her, trust our connection, and learn to trust this new version of myself as well. I had to let go to an extent and go with the flow rather than attempt to control the situation, which ushered me into a sense of spiritual and emotional maturity and made me a better horsewoman. Once I was able to let go of my own agenda and become a pure and clear channel, I was able to learn about the depths of partnership and experience a profound connection with my horse.

You may have felt an intrinsic connection with various animals throughout your lifetime, or there may be a select few that stand out in your mind. Regardless, those bonds are very important. As our partners, animals are here to form relationships that can enrich and shape our lives in ways we could never fully imagine. They are ready to connect deeply with us as long as we are willing to share the experience.

## Reflections

Reflect on an animal with whom you've felt a deep connection or sense of oneness, either recently or in the distant past.

1. Who was that animal? What was their name?
2. What was the connection like for you, and how did it feel special?
3. What impact did this partnership have on you?

## Exercise: Opening the Connection

One of the founding principles of connecting to the souls of animals and communicating with them is acknowledging our inherent oneness with them. Seeing animals, and all of life, as an extension of ourselves is a sacred key to understanding them. To do this successfully, we must be able to release any judgments, prejudices, or feelings of superiority over other beings—even on an unconscious level. This enables us to connect, feel, and understand the wisdom they have to share with us.

The following exercise can be done as a visualization or meditation. Often, students tell me they can't visualize or are not good at meditating; if you feel that way, simply read through the following exercise (and future ones in this book) with the intention that you are participating in, taking on, and embodying what is being shared. Pretend, even. Then take a few moments at the end of the exercise and allow the intended frequency to filter into your consciousness, knowing that this will happen organically. Not being able to visualize or meditate is not a reason to dismiss the exercises in this book; participating in them is a small step, which in the end will lead to awakening and transformation.

This exercise will help set you up for a successful connection with the animals.

1. Prepare a space as free from noise and distraction as possible where you can relax, undisturbed.
2. To begin, uncross your arms and legs, straighten your back, and bring yourself into a relaxed and comfortable position—either sitting or lying down.
3. Close your eyes if you're comfortable doing so.
4. Take a couple of deep, cleansing breaths, inhaling through the nose and exhaling through the mouth. As you breathe in, visualize breathing in universal white light healing energy and exhaling any cares, worries, fears, or doubts you may have.
5. Now, I'd like you to visualize yourself sitting in a beautiful spot out in nature, possibly at a familiar location.
6. Connect with or imagine the beating of your heart.
7. Visualize or imagine that Mother Earth also has a heartbeat. Now, visualize or imagine your heartbeat

synching up with the heartbeat of Mother Earth. Some of you may want to visualize or imagine this heartbeat as the beating of a drum.

8. Now visualize or imagine your heartbeat and the heartbeat of Mother Earth synching up with the heartbeat of every living being in the universe. First with all the two-legged beings, then with all the four-legged beings, now with the winged ones, now with all the water beings, and finally with the insects, reptiles, and any other living being. Take your time with this step.

9. Feel the harmony and connection stemming from this unified heartbeat.

10. Call forth any judgments, prejudices, or feelings of superiority over other beings you may have, whether conscious or not, and trust that they will surface for you. Thank them for the role they played in your life as you prepare to release them.

11. Visualize gathering them into a large, invisible helium ball that you are holding out in front of you. On the count of three, release this ball of unnecessary concepts and beliefs to be transmuted by the universe.

12. Notice how you feel after releasing them.

13. Now send love out to Mother Earth and to all the beings you connected with via your synched heartbeats. Then visualize or feel the love coming back to you tenfold.

14. Ask and intend that you can bring this feeling or state back at will.

15. Open your eyes and return to the present, knowing
    that you are now connected to all of life.

You can revisit this exercise anytime you feel the need for a
reconnection. Eventually, it will become second nature and part
of your consciousness.

## Chapter 2
# Experiencing a Deep Bond

*Dogs are not our whole life, but they make our lives whole.*
~ROGER CARAS

Scorpia was the fifth puppy of seven in her litter and was so named because she was born under the sign of Scorpio, known for being emotional, imaginative, and intense. Blessed with incredible willpower and tenacity, Scorpios usually succeed at whatever they choose to do. It was no surprise to her person and soul mate, Shelley, that the name is also used for a sentry in the animated series *She-Ra: Princess of Power*, because Scorpia soon became a powerful sentry for Shelley, an ally and companion in everything she did.

"Scorpia was beautiful from her very first breath," Shelley remembers. "And from the first moment of her life, I knew she was mine. It couldn't have been otherwise—Scorpio is a passionate water sign whose strength is derived from the psychic and emotional realms. Like its fellow water signs, Cancer and Pisces, Scorpio is intuitively and clairvoyantly inclined. Scorpia was all of that and much more."

Shelley's son's dog was Scorpia's mama, and the delivery of the litter took place in the family's huge walk-in closet, carefully watched over by both Shelley and her son. Though there were seven pups to choose from, from the moment the fifth pup emerged, Shelley had no doubt that this was the one she wanted to keep. While there was nothing in her appearance to make her stand out from her brothers and sisters, Shelley felt an instant connection, like a light shining from inside the tiny pup that she was irresistibly drawn to. Shelley immediately cradled Scorpia in her arms, and as the tiny pup snuggled against her, she felt deep in her heart that there was a special connection between them.

Under Shelley's care, Scorpia grew up to be a sturdy rottweiler who always received compliments on how strong, beautiful, and healthy she looked. Scorpia and Shelley lived together on five acres just outside Kansas City, Kansas, and they shared a glorious life together, with Scorpia's face always illuminated by that big rottweiler smile of pure joy. Even when she was sleeping, Scorpia seemed to radiate happiness and contentment.

They quickly became a team, whether they were taking rides, going for walks, or just relaxing at home together. As active as Scorpia was, she also loved curling up on the couch in the evening with Shelley, her head in Shelley's lap as Shelley watched TV or read a book.

As long as Shelley had Scorpia next to her, she never felt afraid. Scorpia could read people well, and if she felt someone's ill intent, she would give them a look—that's all it took for them to know not to mess with Shelley. But while she could look mean to strangers, at heart, Scorpia was kind and gentle and would never hurt a soul. In fact, she would gladly play with the neighboring children in the gentlest, most loving fashion. She was even known to allow them to dress her up or make her participate in tea parties with them. It was quite simple—if Shelley was there,

Scorpia was happy, and if Scorpia was around, Shelley was happy. They were true soul mates.

"I can still see her riding in the truck with her head out the window," Shelley reminisces, "her ears flapping in the wind and the biggest smile on her face as we rode on the dirt roads near our house." Scorpia was equally happy when they were at home. "There's a spot on our property," continues Shelley, "where she loved to lie in the sun, watching over the fields and keeping an eye out. Whenever she saw me coming, she came racing toward me at full speed with that smile all over her face. Always the smile."

Scorpia loved to fetch—she had a favorite ball, an orange one that Shelley had bought her for Christmas when she was still just a small pup. Whenever Shelley strolled out of the house and approached Scorpia's favorite spot, she would dash behind a clump of trees that overhung a pond and emerge with her favorite ball in her mouth, ready to play. Smile in place, she would rush up to Shelley and drop the ball at her feet eagerly.

"One hot afternoon," Shelley recalls, "Scorpia brought me the ball and we began to play. I must have been feeling strong that day, because I ended up throwing the ball a little too far. It flew past the tree line into a small stream at the edge of our property. Scorpia dashed after the ball and vanished, disappearing out of sight to retrieve her ball before it could float away.

"I knew she would be gone a while, but as time passed, I began to worry. I could hear her splashing about, but it felt like a long time without seeing her. After several minutes pacing back and forth, I sat down to wait. It must have been a record-setting day for Kansas—not a cloud in the sky, the sun beating down mercilessly, the air hot as an oven, dust rising up in slow-moving clouds and coating everything.

"When Scorpia finally trotted back from the stream and brought her ball to me, her tail was still wagging enthusiastically. She shook the damp from the stream off in a spray of drops that cascaded over me, cool on my hot skin. She looked full of energy, her wet coat glistening in the sun, enthusiasm written large across her face as she looked back and forth from me to the ball. I frowned. 'You want to do that again?' I asked. Scorpia padded the ground, step, step, step, her front legs moving energetically. I wouldn't normally have let her run around too much in that kind of heat, but she was cool from the stream, so I figured as long as I kept throwing it into the stream, she would be fine."

"Here goes nothing," Shelley said as she tossed the ball into the stream once more. Again, Scorpia dashed after it, disappearing into the bushes that lined the creek in pursuit of her beloved ball. Shelley could hear her splashing around as she waited for her. She soon reemerged from the stream with the ball in her mouth. She'd never shown that much interest in the stream before, but having discovered it, Scorpia was now clearly loving it.

"That became our game," says Shelley, "and it seemed to mean a lot to Scorpia. It was clearly good exercise for her, and I enjoyed sitting in the shade waiting for her to appear—wet, happy, and triumphant. Scorpia always let me know when she'd had enough, and true to form, after chasing the ball a half dozen times, she dropped the ball a couple of yards in front of me, then came to lie down beside me in the shade. I looked down at her. 'Want to fetch?' I asked. She shook her head from side to side. 'Sure?' Again, she shook her head. Scorpia was done playing for the day."

That wasn't Scorpia's only game. Shelley used to enjoy running on the dirt roads around her property, and Scorpia always came along with her. Shelley always felt completely safe with Scorpia beside her, and it gave them both the opportunity to get out and explore the local area. Scorpia also loved riding in the truck with Shelley, perched up on the front seat, either looking ahead attentively or with her head out the window, catching the breeze. She was a great companion, and Shelley never felt lonely.

One day, when she was a little over ten years old, Scorpia decided to chase the local barn cat, her fierce rival. She took off like a shot and disappeared around the corner of the barn. At first, Shelley thought nothing of it—she'd done it a hundred times before—but when Scorpia didn't come to Shelley's call, she began to worry that something was wrong. She called her three or four times with no response, then went to look for her. Scorpia wasn't anywhere around the barn, and Shelley was concerned by the time she eventually found Scorpia sitting in the middle of the driveway, just looking at Shelley. She called her again, but Scorpia didn't move—she was unable to walk.

Shelley quickly took off her shirt, wrapped it across Scorpia's tummy in front of her back legs to make a sling, and together they made a slow, arduous journey back up to the house, Scorpia hop, hop, hopping along on two legs. She leaned against Shelley the whole way, clearly grateful for the help. Shelley knew at that moment things had changed forever. She cried for hours that night.

After that day, things slowed down for both of them. Walks took far longer, her favorite ball lay abandoned in the bushes, and Scorpia would limp when she was in pain. She hung in there, though, was still Shelley's constant companion, and always had her smile—but she was never the same physically. Dr. Thomas, her veterinarian, finally offered her some pain meds, which helped a little, but it was clear that she would never be the robust, energetic dog she had been in her prime.

Scorpia had developed a thing for Dr. Thomas. Although she didn't like the vet's office, he won her over with his kindness, and they formed a strong connection. Whenever he came into the room, she'd go up to him and lean against his leg while he'd rub her ears and tell her she was his favorite rottweiler. One day, Shelley pulled into the vet's parking lot, but when she went around to get Scorpia out, Scorpia flat-out refused; she wouldn't budge. Eventually, Dr. Thomas did his whole exam in the front seat of the truck. "It was awkward," says Shelley. "But they loved each other, and it showed."

As he finished his examination, Dr. Thomas's face turned serious, and he began to prepare Shelley for the inevitable fact that Scorpia's time with her might be running short. Three months before Scorpia turned eleven, Shelley knew it was time. Scorpia's quality of life was diminishing, her pain was constant, and so with the deepest of dread, Shelley called and scheduled Dr. Thomas to come out two days later.

"It was the hardest, saddest two days of my life," Shelley recalls. "I put my mattress on the floor and slept next to her both nights to absorb every second of her energy." Scorpia seemed to find comfort in Shelley's arms, but Shelley could sense how much pain she was in. Two days later, when the vet came to visit, Shelley knew she had made the right decision.

The dreaded hour approached, and Dr. Thomas arrived on time at Shelley's home, the needed supplies in his bag. He was a compassionate man who shared Shelley's love for Scorpia, and despite her own gut-wrenching emotional pain, she could sense his solemn sadness for his role. They decided to set up outside on the lawn, in one of Scorpia's favorite spots overlooking the pond. The vet laid down a soft blanket and helped Shelley bring Scorpia outside for the last time.

They settled her comfortably on the blanket, and after allowing some quiet time, the vet administered a relaxant to aid in the process. When Shelley was ready, Dr. Thomas then administered the final shot, and Scorpia's heart slowed down and eventually stopped beating. In that moment, Shelley noticeably felt Scorpia's spirit leave her body, and with that, she felt a piece of her own heart and spirit leave, too. She was overcome with intense emotion; it was so strong that it created a physical pain in her own heart, something she'd never experienced before.

After Scorpia passed, Shelley recalls, "I had never felt such heartbreak. I was lost without my beautiful companion, and I cried daily for months." She felt trapped in a cycle of sadness and depression, unable to move forward, everything around the house a constant reminder of her beloved Scorpia.

Then one day, Shelley read online about my ability to communicate with animals, even those who had crossed over. "Although it was not something I'd generally consider, something in the article resonated with me," says Shelley. "Just thinking about it lifted my spirits and gave me hope." Shelley wasn't sure whether she was acting out of desperation, but she knew she had to email me immediately to schedule a reading, thinking that if I could connect with Scorpia in spirit form, she was fully open to the communication. "I didn't dare tell anyone, lest they thought I'd truly lost it, but I felt such a strong pull to have a session and knew in my heart that for me it was the right thing to do."

On the day of the reading, Shelley first asked me if Scorpia was okay. I told her that Scorpia was sitting right next to her, that she was fine and very happy. Scorpia also shared that she wanted Shelley to be happy, too, something that had felt impossible for Shelley since her passing. Scorpia was very communicative, so I was able to describe her personality quirks, her likes and dislikes, the depth and importance of their relationship, and the lessons Scorpia had come to impart.

Shelley couldn't believe the immediate comfort and relief she felt upon hearing these details about her precious companion. She knew that I truly did have a connection with Scorpia and that she was still with her in spirit, hearing Shelley when she spoke to her. I also let Shelley know that Scorpia was still enjoying rides in the truck with her. "I immediately felt a burden lifting from me, like rain clouds chased away by a strong wind. I left our session with a deep sense of relief and a peace in my heart I hadn't felt since Scorpia was alive and thriving."

Shelley also learned that Scorpia wanted to thank her for giving her such a good life as well as the greatest gift one can give a cherished animal friend: the gift of ending her suffering when it was clear that she couldn't continue on as she was. Through our session, she learned that she and Scorpia had been through many lifetimes together, and that Scorpia was now her guardian angel, available whenever she needed her. I also reassured Shelley that they'd be together again.

"I can't begin to describe the relief and the love I felt," Shelley says. "I didn't want the session to end, and I cried daily for a few weeks afterward, but these were tears of joy."

Shelley still keeps Scorpia's dog collar on her rearview mirror to remind her that Scorpia is always riding beside her in life and in the truck, her head hanging out the window with that big rottweiler smile on her face. Always that smile ...

## Lesson

At times, we may recognize an instant and infallible connection with an animal that catches us off guard. We may not know exactly what it is that draws us to one another, but we recognize that something intangible and compelling is there, something that makes us instantly bond with, fall in love with, and feel that immediate "soul mate" connection with them. This deep bond is divinely inspired by the universe (God or Spirit—whatever your specific belief) and felt deeply within our souls, and if we follow through, it will surely be a highly rewarding and fulfilling experience for both the animal and for us. Sometimes, this can happen with an animal that isn't ours or that we don't have the option to spend a lot of time with, but the experience can still have a profound, even life-changing impact on us. In some cases, circumstances do transpire to allow us to be together—but that isn't always necessary, as animals partner with us in all sorts of ways. It's most important to recognize the partnership for what it is and enjoy it while at the same time being open to the deeper teachings it may bring you.

For Shelley, she recognized that not only was Scorpia highly intuitive, but she could be confident in her wisdom—the wisdom of Scorpia—and relax into that knowledge, connection, and intuition. Shelley felt safe with Scorpia around, trusting the dog's instincts to protect her and keep her aware of things going on around them.

Beyond that connection, however, was the spiritual connection that transcends the physical plane. Shelley became aware of her continuing connection with Scorpia even though she's no longer with her in physical form—but Scorpia guides, protects, and loves Shelley even from the other side. Once Shelley learned this, she realized she could relax once more into the guiding presence that Scorpia provides, resulting from their deep connection that's stronger than death and physical bounds.

When we experience a similar instant connection with an animal, it's important to recognize it, appreciate it, and use it to learn and grow—spiritually, emotionally, and in every way possible.

## Reflections

Reflect on an animal with whom you've felt a deep familiarity right from day one, like they were meant to be yours, and who became a significant friend and ally in your life.

1. What made this connection so special for you?
2. What synchronicities (seeming "coincidences" that aligned) brought you together?
3. Was there a significance in terms of the timing of this partnership?

## Exercise: Linking Energy Fields

Every living being has an energy field. Linking to the energy field of an animal helps us recognize our familiarity with them and connect to them on a deeper level. For simplicity, we are going to discuss just one component of the energy field here: the subtle bodies. Also known as the aura, the energy body is made up of layers that lie just outside the physical body, one over the other, like Russian nested dolls. The energetic layers that comprise the subtle body are the etheric double, the emotional body, the mental body, and the spiritual body.

I think of the energy body or energy field as an extension of who we are and a place where one can connect with and tap into a being. I find it helpful for animal communication to visualize the coming together of both our own energy field and the energy field of an animal with whom we'd like to connect.

Here is an exercise to help you do that:

1. Prepare a space as free from noise and distraction as possible where you can relax, undisturbed.

2. To begin, uncross your arms and legs, straighten your back, and bring yourself into a relaxed and comfortable position—either sitting or lying down.

3. Close your eyes if you're in a position to do so.

4. Take a couple of deep, cleansing breaths, inhaling through the nose and exhaling through the mouth. As you breathe in, visualize breathing in universal white light healing energy and exhaling any cares, worries, fears, or doubts you may have.

5. Now, I'd like you to visualize your energy field or aura as an orb around you that encompasses your physical body plus an extra three to six feet around you.

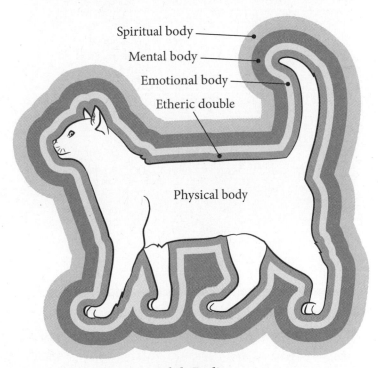

Spiritual body

Mental body

Emotional body

Etheric double

Physical body

**Subtle Bodies**

6. Next, I'd like you to visualize one of your animal companions that is currently living, and visualize their energy field or aura as an orb around them. This orb encompasses their physical body plus an extra one to six feet around them, depending on the species. Kittens and small animals have smaller energy fields, and horses and large animals have larger ones.

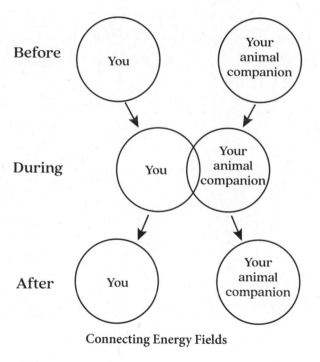

**Connecting Energy Fields**

7. Now, in your mind's eye, visualize or think of the two energy fields (yours and theirs) as similar-size circles in front of you.

8. Have them move together until a portion of each of them is overlapping. This portion will make up roughly

a third of each energy field; this is the place where your energy fields come together and you connect.

9. Notice how you feel when connected to your animal friend.

10. See if you receive any impressions—thoughts, feelings, colors, images, or messages—and make note of them.

11. When ready, visualize or think of the two energy fields moving apart from one another so that there is no overlap and each field is left separate and whole. Disconnecting is good energy hygiene, so neither being is left energetically burdened by the other.

12. Open your eyes and return to the present, knowing that you now have an important step in linking up with an animal.

You now have a method of connecting with the energy field of an animal friend.

# Chapter 3
# A Divine Appointment

*All creatures exist for a purpose.*
*Even an ant knows what that purpose is—*
*not with its brain, but somehow it knows.*

~LAME DEER, SEEKER OF VISIONS

"Nagi, come!"

Silence.

"Nagi, come!"

No response. All Asia could remember hearing was the wind whistling gently as it rolled off the lake into the trees and the *whoosh* of rushing blood in her ears. Biting back the bile that was roiling in her stomach, she had done her best not to panic. She couldn't have lost her precious Nagi, could she?

The adventure had begun in Boston. With her BA from the University of New Hampshire in hand and boyfriend Mike in tow, Asia had decided to leave stuffy old New England behind and seek purpose and enlightenment under the big skies out west. She said farewell to her spiritual mentor—her mom, a psychic who ran a metaphysical bookstore—and started to pack their rainbow-colored Volkswagen van, a psychedelic interpretation of some-one's hallucinations. They were happy, free, unconcerned how they might appear to the world, and determined to live according to the spiritual principles Asia had recently been studying. Her mentor had recently become a follower of John Fire Lame Deer, a Miniconjou Lakota, and gifted Asia with the book *Lame Deer, Seeker of Visions*. Asia placed her copy proudly on the dashboard of the van, her guide to all matters spiritual, ready at hand whenever she needed it.

The day before they were due to head west out of Durham on NH 4, they stopped by their local gas station to fill the tank and check the tires and oil one last time.

While Mike gassed up the car, Asia wandered into a pet store. The light inside was dim, and while her eyes adjusted, she stood and listened to the sounds of the various animals mewing and snuffling and shifting in the shadows. As her eyes gradually focused, she could see a cardboard box nudged up against a set of metal bars. She guessed it was to protect the pets from too much handling, but to her eyes, it looked like a jail. She peered into the box; it was filled with a tumbled mass of kittens, all ears and eyes and soft mewing.

Asia guessed they might be Siamese from the masked nature of their darker coats on the face, but her eyes were quickly drawn to one of the kittens, who scrambled tenaciously past its twin and over its littermates to reach her. Asia felt powerless to resist as she reached her fingers through the bars toward the little kitten. As it snuggled against her fingers, Asia felt a jolt of electricity run up her arm and into her body, settling into a warm feeling deep in the pit of her stomach.

Even though they were about to leave town, Asia felt that something within her had changed when she and the kitten had connected. She had been recently told by her mentor, "You are an animal person," and Asia knew her attraction to animals to be part of her nature. But staring into the blue eyes of this tiny white kitten made Asia wonder if she had found her spirit animal. Sometimes these beings travel through life with an individual, assisting and guiding them much the same way a guardian angel does, while at other times a spirit guide may come to a person just to assist for a short time. However the spirits worked, Asia stood at the threshold of a critical time in her life. She was on the verge of a new life, heading out west with Mike—was her spirit animal really calling to her at a time like this?

Trying to push such thoughts from her mind, she said nothing to Mike; they drove back to their apartment, which was almost empty in preparation for their trip. But though Asia busied herself with last-minute packing, she couldn't shake the image of the kitten from her mind, couldn't forget the feeling when it had touched her fingertips.

Asia had studied French in college, and the word for what she had been feeling, *angoisse*, beautifully described the trepidations that wracked her soul. In English, they call it angst-ridden, but *angst* seemed such an ugly word for such a beautiful feeling. Asia confessed to Mike what had happened. He grinned, grabbed the car keys, and drove her back to the pet store.

If this was meant to be, Asia needed a sign. She asked the clerk to show them the twin kittens. He pulled the kittens out and handed one to Mike and one to her. Asia knew instinctively that Mike had the one that had snuggled her fingers, and sure enough, the twin Asia got immediately scratched and tried to get away. They traded kittens, and the second one clung to her, purring softly, and wouldn't let her put him down. Asia had found her spirit animal.

Back at their empty apartment, the kitten went off exploring while Asia, pondering a name for her new family member, drifted off to sleep. She slipped easily into a dream state where a being appeared before her. Identifying himself as one of her guides, he informed Asia that the new cat-being in her life wished to be called Nagi. Her guide went on to share that this sweet soul had come to help her awaken further to her own spiritual essence, and she immediately knew, right there in her dream state, that Nagi was his name. Finding the right name for her soul mate was like receiving a shot of adrenaline; Asia awoke and could feel her heart pounding. This was a feeling that could not be faked or invented. Everything simply felt right.

"Where's the kitten?" she asked Mike. He looked around, but the kitten had vanished. Together, they rummaged through the few remaining packing boxes, Mike calling out, "Here, kitty, kitty," but there was no sign of him. Puzzled, Mike grabbed a flashlight and began poking under low places—a chair, a couch—at every moment expecting to find that tiny white kitten with its crossed blue eyes peering out at them, but there was no sign of him.

They were beginning to get worried—the apartment wasn't very big, so there weren't that many places to look—when Asia suddenly blurted out, "Nagi! Come."

Almost instantly, Nagi came dashing around the corner from the kitchenette, his little legs sliding like an ice-skater on the slick wooden floor, and leaped into her lap. He immediately curled up, closed his eyes, and began purring softly.

Mike leaned on the broom, obviously perplexed. "How'd he know?"

"That's his name," Asia said. "He felt it."

Mike nodded. "You know, Asia, I wasn't sure about this," he confessed, "getting a kitten right before we hit the road. But now, seeing the two of you together, it just feels right." He bent over, kissing her cheek. "I think our spiritual journey has begun."

They traveled west on many highways and many roads, sleeping out under the stars with Nagi snuggling in Asia's sleeping bag. He was warm and cuddly against her, his soft fur and steady breathing comforting and soothing, making her feel a peace and fulfillment Asia had never experienced.

After several weeks on the road, they camped in Mendota County Park in Madison, Wisconsin—a beautiful, serene site with shady green trees leading down to a large, tranquil lake.

They spent several days there, doing nothing more energetic than soaking up the warm sun and swimming in the cool waters, the days drifting by in a relaxed haze. Eventually, it was time to hit the road again. It didn't take them long to pack their meager possessions into the rainbow van. As Mike closed up the back, Asia looked around for Nagi. She hadn't seen him for a while, but Asia wasn't worried; he was always close, always showed up as soon as Asia called.

"Nagi, come!"

Asia perched on the passenger seat of the van and leafed through *Lame Deer, Seeker of Visions* as she waited, but after a couple of minutes, Nagi had still not appeared.

"Nagi, come!" Asia called again.

Silence.

"Nagi, come!"

Unable to accept the silence that met her, Asia was becoming frantic. Somehow Nagi had disappeared from their campsite. Any plans to leave were immediately abandoned. They spent the rest of the day scouring the site, calling, "Nagi, come! Nagi, come." Total strangers heard their calls and came to join in, helping search for their precious Siamese kitten. The big, beautiful lake had become an ominous body of water, a dangerous place for a kitten. Canoeists and kayakers searched the shoreline while campers and RVers walked the woods, calling Nagi in every language one could imagine. There were so many miles to search, so many places a kitten could get lost or hurt, so many potential predators in the acres around the campsite.

But though their calls of "Nagi, come!" brought only silence, Asia sensed in her heart that the unconditional love they shared, their spiritual unity, would triumph. Quite simply, Asia could feel Nagi's presence even though she couldn't see him.

Up until then, they had been so innocent. They had gazed up at the beauty of the Milky Way, Nagi lying peacefully on her chest, and dreamed and planned of their new life, of all the wonderful things they would do.

Such peace!

Then, suddenly, their spiritual journey had become a train wreck.

Asia was desperate, but she was not ready to give up. They drove into town, put advertisements in all the newspapers in Madison—*Wisconsin State Journal*, *Badger Herald*, *Capital Times*, *Daily Cardinal*—and used her dad's office number as a way for people to get in touch. While they waited for someone—anyone—to contact them, they fasted and focused on connecting to spirit with the intention of cleansing their hearts and letting Nagi know they were looking for him and that they would be reunited. Every evening, Asia drove into town and called her dad's office, but day after day passed without any response. Asia knew Nagi was still alive, knew he was out there searching for her, but she had to confess that with each passing day, her hopes dipped a little further. She and Mike even began to discuss the possibility that they may have to consider moving on, despite Asia's desperation to wait until they found Nagi. "We can't stay in Madison forever, after all," Mike said, and Asia couldn't disagree.

On the seventh day, Asia lay outside sunning, trying to reach out to Nagi with her mind. It was a beautiful late summer's day, not a cloud in the sky, and as Asia gazed upward, she spotted a red-tailed hawk drifting lazily on the currents. It circled above her once, twice, three times, four times, then turned and headed west. In some cultures, a red-tailed hawk is believed to possess exceptionally acute vision, and when one flies close by, individuals can sometimes experience precognitive dreams—visions in which they are able to see the future.

As the hawk circled over her, Asia found her head filled with a strange vision of Nagi with her father back in Boston. Asia sat up, looking around, trying to figure it out. Her father was one of the least intuitive people you could ever meet, so it was not him calling out to her. Asia knew right there and then that she had to call her dad's secretary, Judy, who was fielding messages in response to their ad.

There were no cell phones back then, so with her heart racing, they drove into town, crammed a handful of quarters into a pay phone, and dialed.

"Asia? Is that you?" Judy asked as she picked up the phone. "You won't believe this, but a lady in Madison just called me and said she found Nagi."

Asia gasped, tears welling up in her eyes. "Are you sure?"

"She seemed very certain," said Judy. "Her husband found him and brought him home, and his wife had seen your ad, so she called me right away. She said when they call Nagi by his name, he comes running."

Judy called the lady back, and they said they would bring Nagi to the campground right away.

When they got back, the lady was already there, waiting for them. As Asia jumped out of the car and ran toward them,

Nagi leaped out of the woman's hands and jumped into Asia's arms, burying his face into her neck. Her tears ran down his soft white fur, but Asia didn't care. They had found each other. Nagi wouldn't let go for days, and Asia wouldn't let him out of her sight.

Once Asia had Nagi back, she felt as though she had a new perspective on things. They had headed west on a spiritual journey, but they hadn't truly embraced it until Nagi disappeared. But now, after a week of fasting, praying, and sacred ceremonies, and with Nagi back in her arms, Asia found that she could now see auras around animals and easily connect to other animal guides. The red-tailed hawk had recognized the spiritual power Nagi and Asia shared, a magical relationship that lasted throughout the twenty years they spent together.

From that day on, they were never apart, not even when Asia left him with trusted friends for the two years she spent in Paris. They talked daily. They didn't need the phone; Asia just reached out to Nagi and knew that he heard her. Nagi knew Asia was still there, still loving him, and would see him again soon.

Eventually, they settled in one of the most wonderful places on Earth: Taos, New Mexico, a place that embodies the endless spiritual journey that continues beyond the mortal existence. The very light there is spiritual, cradled in the Sangre de Cristo Mountains that have inspired countless artists, healers, musicians, and writers.

Nagi protected Asia through many failed relationships and comforted her after the sudden deaths of her parents—father in a car crash, mother from a sudden illness. Both parents passed so suddenly that Asia never went through the grieving process, never felt she had proper completion. They were just gone.

But when Nagi's final days approached, he was able to give her that sacred experience. He spent seven days in her arms, drifting in and out, finally offering *her* the chance to protect him. Nagi had always protected Asia, allowing her to draw comfort and strength from him for twenty wonderful years, and now, at the end, Asia was able to repay him. When he finally passed in the middle of the night, it was not the end for them; it was simply a new beginning.

After Nagi passed, he came to Asia from the spirit realm. He told her he had initially incarnated into Nagi's body to teach her unconditional love, and that he has always been with her from the beginning of time—her main spirit guide who sits on her left shoulder and watches over her. Not a day goes by that Asia doesn't miss him, but she takes comfort that he is still with her whether she calls on him or not.

"Nagi, come."

## Lesson

Sometimes we might feel like we simply know something, but we don't know how we know it or where it came from. That's because it's been imparted to us through divine wisdom. When we are partnered with and connected to an animal, we often have information about them that we know in the depths of our soul—because they have communicated it to us in one form or another. It may take a bit of stretching or opening your mind to recognize the information you receive as such, but once we get into the practice of receiving this type of information, we are able to notice more readily when it appears. When we pay attention to those occurrences, we will realize that we're more deeply connected to the animal than we may have thought possible, and this will facilitate further communication between our souls.

For this to happen, it's imperative to pay attention to signs and synchronicities—little (or sometimes big) nuggets from the universe that teach us something about ourselves and our paths. Oftentimes, we may notice synchronicities in our lives—for example, seeing the same word, phrase, or message from multiple sources—but we may not immediately know what to do with them. The more we are mindful of these signs and aware of the spiritual connections in our lives, the more we'll recognize divine guidance from the universe. Thankfully, Asia was able to see the signs in her own life and utilize them to not only partner with her precious Nagi, but then to get him back. Her intuition and connection with him helped them both out in myriad ways, allowing them to spend Nagi's entire life together and enrich each other's lives deeply.

It's important to remember to trust your own truth, your connection, and the universe. Sometimes it's in those tiny signs and synchronicities where we discover the greatest of wisdom.

## Reflections

Reflect on a time when you first met with an animal and felt a deep visceral sensation—a feeling that you were meant to be together.

1. What physical sensations did you feel?
2. Were there times when you felt you knew something about your animal but didn't know how you knew it?
3. How did that connection fuel your inner knowing and certainty?

## Exercise: Deepening Your Connection

One of the first steps to deepening our partnership with an animal friend involves releasing the noise and busyness around us and learning to go within. Being "grounded," or connected to Mother Earth, gives us a wonderful starting point when it comes to mastering this.

The process I'll guide you through below also connects you to the energies of the cosmos, or Father Sky. Being connected to these energies, both above and below, sets the stage perfectly within you for a successful connection with an animal companion.

Grounding is a vitally important step in preparing ourselves to tune in with the animals. It makes us feel solid, peaceful, and very present in our bodies. It also enables us to connect with our animal companions at a much deeper level.

When we are grounded, the animals resonate with, trust, and open up to us naturally and willingly, and it becomes far easier for us to partner with them.

I introduce the crown chakra in this exercise. In case you've never heard of chakras, they are simply energy portals—sometimes referred to as wheels of light or wheels of life—located in various positions throughout the body. They are the vehicles through which we receive and assimilate universal life force energy. Any vortex of activity within the energy field can be called a chakra, but I will refer to the seven major chakras: root, sacral, solar plexus, heart, throat, third eye (or brow), and crown.

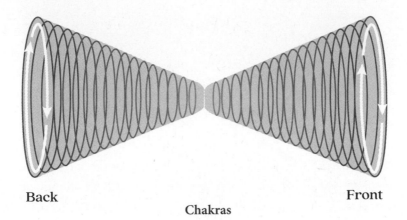

**Back**

**Front**

**Chakras**

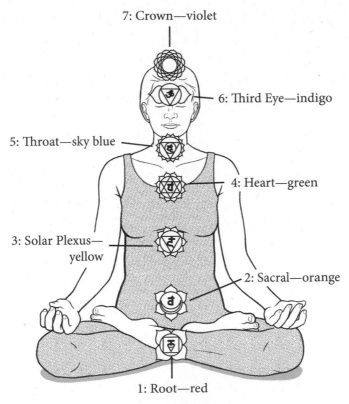

7: Crown—violet

6: Third Eye—indigo

5: Throat—sky blue

4: Heart—green

3: Solar Plexus—
yellow

2: Sacral—orange

1: Root—red

**Chakra Anatomy**

Chakras are cone-shaped and spin and emanate outward, drawing in and filtering that vital life force energy through our beings. Just like it sounds, the crown chakra is located at the top of the head. It is the chakra that opens us up to a higher consciousness, allowing us to access insights and ideas beyond our current perception and vision. Working with your crown chakra is important in learning to connect with animals, as it will not only open your mind to new concepts, but it clears the way to opening your other chakras as well.

The following exercise can be done as a visualization or meditation—or, if you don't feel confident that you can do either of those options, simply go through the exercise and pretend or act as if you are doing it (you will still receive benefits from doing it this way).

1. Prepare a space as free from noise and distraction as possible where you can relax, undisturbed.

2. To begin, uncross your arms and legs, straighten your back, and bring yourself into a relaxed and comfortable position—either sitting or lying down.

3. Take a couple of deep, cleansing breaths, inhaling through the nose and exhaling through the mouth. As you breathe in, visualize breathing in universal white light healing energy and exhaling any cares, worries, fears, or doubts you may have.

4. Now, visualize a beam of white light coming down from above, toward the top of your head (the location of your crown chakra). Visualize it entering there, slowly coming down through your body and filling every cell within you with this white light.

5. Take all the time you need, and when you feel you are filled with this universal healing energy, visualize it exiting from the soles of your feet and the base of your tailbone.

6. Visualize the energy going down through the floor and any floors that may be below you, connecting you and your energy deep within Mother Earth. Think of it like the connection an oak tree has with the ground: deep, wide, strong, and anchored.

7. Now, consciously feel your feet on the floor and your seat in the chair (if seated) and notice how solid and calm you feel.

8. You are now grounded and connected to the energies from both above (cosmic) and below (earth).

9. Notice how you feel in this moment: physically, emotionally, and mentally.

10. If you have an animal companion nearby, notice how they react to you or seem to feel about you when you're in this state; perhaps they want to be closer to you. They are experts at sensing energy and generally love it when we are connected this way.

11. Set a strong intention that simply by doing this exercise, you are setting the stage for a deeper partnership with your animal companion.

12. Be assured that you can come back to this space often by simply visualizing this feeling and time.

13. Feel gratitude for this process.

14. Feel your feet on the floor, take a couple of conscious breaths, and come back to present awareness.

I encourage you to revisit this exercise often via whichever method you chose to do it and branch out and experiment with some of the other methods.

section two
# Animal Companion as Teacher

# Chapter 4
# Seeing Things
# in a New Way

*If you want to know the end, look at the beginning.*
~AFRICAN PROVERB

In 1993, I adopted an adorable nine-week-old golden retriever puppy I named Jiggs. We were deeply bonded from the first day we met, but within a few short weeks, Jiggs started to fall ill with a variety of ailments.

I took him to my local veterinarian. We soon became regular visitors, and each time, the vet suggested more medication and another vaccination. You name a problem, Jiggs seemed to have it—ear mites, eye infections, stomach problems.

I was sure the veterinarian knew her business, but it seemed to me that Jiggs's constant and varied symptoms were beyond conventional medicine. After many trips to that vet, I realized that Jiggs needed something more than just drugs. While the limited approach to veterinary care wasn't cutting it, I couldn't deny that I felt a stirring in my soul, a hint that there was something I was missing. I was positive there was a deeper meaning for everything we were experiencing, and I longed to see the bigger picture. At the time, it evaded me.

Looking back now, it seems so obvious, but in that hazy moment, it was like a warning bell going off in my head. The future of my lovely dog Jiggs lay in my hands, and I had to do something drastic if he was going to have a long and happy life. It was clear to me that while the allopathic veterinarian was treating his endless list of symptoms, we weren't getting to the underlying cause.

I had long been seeing holistic doctors myself and was studying energy medicine at the time. *Why shouldn't Jiggs benefit, too?* I wondered in a moment of clarity.

After some searching, I found a holistic vet located an hour and a half out of the city. She listened to what I told her and gave Jiggs a thorough head-to-toe examination. Finally, she looked me straight in the eye. "If we don't get this under control," she told me, "he's probably not going to live past the age of five."

As I drove home from that visit, I looked over at Jiggs sitting contentedly on the passenger seat, gazing out the window. On the outside, he looked happy—healthy, even—but the vet's words kept ringing in my ears. Why wasn't my dog getting better? I couldn't help but feel it was a little unfair. It was then I fully realized that it was up to me. I had to be the one to take full responsibility for Jiggs's well-being and, in the process, figure out exactly how to heal him.

I had recently been trained in Body Alignment Technique, a healing modality for humans that was producing great results with my clients. The more I thought about it, the more it seemed like it might be worth trying with Jiggs. The technique is based on the idea that negative emotional experiences can become subconsciously locked into our bodies at a cellular level and, therefore, become part of our biological systems. Body Alignment Technique aims to clear these subconscious memory pathways using vibrational energy to treat and release the source of an imbalance. It not only improves us emotionally, mentally, and spiritually, but it can also correct physical imbalances, leaving the recipient feeling grounded, deeply connected, and in balance.

*If stress can cause these reactions in humans, why not in animals?* I wondered. Every day and every moment, we are exposed to stress in some form, which can impact our body, mind, and spirit. To my delight, Jiggs responded quickly to the Body Alignment Technique treatments, as well as the rest of the regime I had him on, and his health returned rapidly. He had more energy, his ailments quickly cleared up, and he soon became the happy, healthy dog with the shiny coat that I had always imagined him to be.

As I watched him change before my very eyes, I began to realize that Jiggs had come into my life for a reason. He was there to teach me to follow my intuition and heart in all things, just as I had followed them to restore his health. This was an earth-shaking revelation for me. I was amazed I hadn't seen it clearly before; I'd largely kept my business life separate from my spiritual life, and yet the two were merging before my eyes. As I strove to get Jiggs healthy, I was also taking the first tentative steps on a new career path that took the energy work I was already trained in and performing on humans and adapted it to work with animals. This was not something I had even considered possible before, but I felt certain that if I had thought of it, I'd surely have wanted to do it.

To my surprise, not only did I get immense personal satisfaction from working with animals, my business also took off. Jiggs had reawakened a magic within me that I'd forgotten about, and it changed my life. The more I explored my rediscovered passion and newfound connection, the more I sensed Jiggs nudging and urging me toward it. His energy seemed to diminish anytime I worked on real estate, and I could sense an uplift of positive energy as I studied and pursued animal communication and healing. The closer I got to my life's mission, the more relaxed and fulfilled he seemed to be.

As Jiggs rebounded to a healthy specimen of a golden retriever puppy, I dived into becoming a determined, unwavering animal intuitive and energy healer, just as he was nudging me to do. Of course, my skills grew gradually stronger over the years—not just from my growing practice, but also from years of studying courses in animal communication and every other modality I could get my hands on as well as my own experiences with Jiggs. The fulfillment I experienced far outweighed any enjoyment of my previous career.

In the meantime, I began to build my new business. One of the first steps I took was to train with another animal communicator, a person who learned from Penelope Smith, the founding pioneer of animal communication—or, as she calls it, interspecies telepathic communication. I drove a couple of hours west from Toronto to Stratford, Ontario, for a weekend.

Filled with trepidation, I wasn't sure what to expect from the training as I began to ask a pony a list of questions supplied by the teacher. To my delight, we had a true conversation—I asked, and he answered me telepathically! It was an amazing experience that I'll never forget.

Later in the weekend, we assembled in another part of the barn to exchange pictures of one of our own animal companions with fellow students to try our hands at "distance communication." To my dismay, I realized I'd forgotten Jiggs's picture (and this was long before smartphones). I couldn't believe it; he was the center of my universe.

Thankfully, the teacher was prepared with a stack of photos of animals that had volunteered to help students learn to communicate with them. Just as I was nearing the end of the stack, the one that jumped out at me was a gray Andalusian stallion, a beautiful purebred from the Iberian Peninsula. "That's Lucero," the teacher informed me. "He's incredibly special."

Just how special he was, neither of us could have imagined. Lucero's full story appears later in chapter 7, but for now, the important thing to note is that selecting that photo—and my subsequent communication with Lucero—changed my life forever. It felt as though I had opened a ten-ton silo of magic.

Lucero felt very familiar to me, like a long-lost relative. The first thing he said to me was that he knew Jiggs. Imagine my surprise! It's a foreign concept to us that one being could know another despite never having met them, but in the spirit realm, all beings are aware of each other. This fact immediately made me feel bonded to Lucero, and I could sense thousands of years' worth of knowledge and ancient wisdom in his spirit. Both Lucero and Jiggs ended up being very instrumental in my learning of human-animal communication, my career path, and the process of deep enlightenment and friendship that followed.

As I learned and grew, I began to feel more and more fulfilled, as if I were finally on the most purposeful path for my life. Talking to animals resonated within my heart, as though it was what I had been meant to do all along. At the same time, my real estate career was quickly losing its luster despite the fact that it was going the best it ever had, and I longed for warmer weather and my spiritual home. Not knowing exactly what drew me there other than the urgings of Jiggs and a higher calling, I traveled to Sedona, Arizona, to recharge my batteries—Jiggs in tow, of course. Jiggs tolerated the travel quite well, sleeping comfortably in the back seat and settling down on his blanket each night in the latest hotel room, waiting patiently for my return while I went to grab dinner.

Jiggs and I liked it so much, we ended up traveling back and forth several times for extended stays until finally moving there several years later. The conversations I had during this and many other cross-country journeys with Jiggs would fill a thick journal. But it's not so much the travel I recall as the countless walks. I can still remember Jiggs discovering that the red rocks and canyons around Sedona had no grass on which to relieve himself— he tried raising his leg on a cactus, but once was enough to teach him that wasn't a good idea. From then on, whenever he came upon a cactus, he would glower at it before moving on to a more suitable location.

Meanwhile, Jiggs became the picture of vibrant good health, his early travails behind him. As he matured, his character matched the alpha dog stereotype and then some. But though he stood tall and handsome, he never initiated aggression toward another animal. Most other dogs instinctively sensed that Jiggs should not be messed with, and on the rare occasion when another dog mistakenly chose to attack Jiggs, the encounter was always short-lived. Jiggs seemed to stand even taller while the other dog slouched away, licking its wounds.

Not that Jiggs was always noble. As a puppy, he had loved to curl up around the cool base of a porcelain toilet, but as he grew, he soon became too big to fit comfortably around it. Jiggs clearly blamed the toilet, barking at it incessantly to show it who was boss.

Jiggs was a pedigree golden retriever with a lineage that included a long string of titles. As a result, Jiggs and the rest of his litter had been trained to swim when they were mere babies. Consequently, anytime Jiggs wasn't on a leash, he'd head for the nearest body of water, leaping in with that pure joy that characterizes a happy dog. Our local area in Sedona includes numerous places to swim, and Jiggs had several favorites, including Red Rock Crossing, Seven Sacred Pools, and West Fork. Despite his dislike of the intense heat—the temperature was 105 degrees Fahrenheit on the day we initially arrived in Arizona—Jiggs acclimated so well between his daily swims and splaying himself out on the cold tile floors at home. His joyous attitude and ability to make himself comfortable no matter the circumstances were a sign to me that he approved of the path I was following.

Toronto winters are cold, dull, wet, and snowy. By comparison, in Sedona, winters are often sunny and dry, with daytime highs in the fifties, even sixties. But the climate is only a fraction of the reason we settled there.

The Northern Arizona region of Sedona is often called Red Rock Country due to the iconic red sandstone monoliths—Cathedral Rock, Coffeepot Rock, and Thunder Mountain—that surround the town of Sedona. When we first moved there, the population was 10,602—I liked to think of that last two representing Jiggs and me. Sedona sits at the center of a twenty-two-mile circumference of mystical energy and has become a well-known spiritual hub in recent decades, with its famed Sedona Vortexes—"power spots" of spiritual energy renowned for healing, meditation, and transformation. Perfect for me and my work.

I remember one day we met a man with a golden retriever on the trails in Sedona. He asked how old Jiggs was. Jiggs was ten at the time but looked more like a four-year-old—lean, muscular, and brimming with energy. As I told him Jiggs's age, I could see his eyes going from dog to dog, trying to figure out how Jiggs could look so much younger and healthier compared to his out-of-shape dog, who was only six years old.

Like clockwork, we would take two long walks each day out on the beautiful red rock trails. One such day, I suddenly noticed Jiggs wasn't in his usual position next to me. Stopping, I turned back to see his gaze fixating skyward, although I couldn't tell why in the bright, cloudless sunlight. Instinctively, I knew before I heard its call—a red-tailed hawk soared above us, reminding me of my horse Jasmine from so many years before. It had come to bless us, and I knew it was also showing me that I was on the right path, that I was being led further toward my purpose that had now become my passion, which is part of what had led me to Sedona in the first place.

Toward the conclusion of Jiggs's time on Earth, his arthritis began to bother him more and more. After much research, I started taking him to the shore of the mighty Pacific Ocean when we'd travel back to British Columbia, where he would swim enthusiastically in the ice-cold salt water. Afterward, he would trot home without any pain or limping, a youthful pep in his step, displaying the incredible benefits of hydrotherapy. What a character!

He had outgrown the toilet, but in those final days, Jiggs would lie down against the cool base of our refrigerator. Not only did it keep him cool, but it also ensured that I never opened the fridge without his knowledge.

As I reflected on Jiggs and his extraordinary life, I thought back to his difficult start and the health trials we went through when he was still young. Like someone illuminating a room, it occurred to me that I had been right, and it had all happened for a very important reason. Jiggs had needed me, yes; most importantly, he had guided my journey toward becoming the person

I am today. Without his ailments and my determination to cure them, I may never have pursued the field of animal communication and healing. Humbly, I realized that he likely arrived here with his burden in order to teach me a whole lot of things that I could in turn teach others. Both Lucero and Jiggs are with me today, and people who receive my training are guided in part by these wonderful animal guides: the spirit of a wise Andalusian stallion and the love of a faithful golden retriever.

Jiggs was on the earthly plane for fourteen and a half happy years, but with a dog like Jiggs, even the end isn't the end. Personally, I don't believe our animal soul mate connections ever end—they go on forever. Jiggs is still with me today in spirit form even though he no longer inhabits his earthly body.

In 2007, just days after he'd crossed over, he came to me in a dream to tell me that he could help a client's dog who had stopped eating, so the following day I called the client and shared what Jiggs had told me. The client said that her dog was with her husband at the bank, but she'd tell him as soon as they came home.

She called me back later, excited, and told me that while they were at the bank, a teller offered their dog a biscuit. Just as he was about to decline the biscuit, her husband noticed that the dog seemed interested. He gave the dog the treat. He ate it. Then another. Then another.

What was it exactly that Jiggs had done to get this dog to eat?

During my dreamtime, he came to me, and it felt just the same as when he had been with me on the physical plane. He had been aware of my work and my clients, and he clearly still was. "I can help this dog," he told me. "I love eating and will eat vicariously through him." Not only was he happy to help, but it also solved a major problem for the client, their dog, and even for me, as I had been working very hard to help this dog to start eating again.

These days, whenever I think of Jiggs, I am reminded of that African proverb:

"If you want to know the end, look at the beginning."

Jiggs was with me in the beginning, and he will be with me until the end.

## Lesson

While it may not be traditional in everyday culture to think of animals as teachers, they clearly are. They can teach us anything from basic principles—such as slowing down to enjoy life—to more complex ones, like following our intuition and trusting ourselves. There is truly a wealth of information animals can teach us when we're willing to learn, and to do that, we must acknowledge their purpose in relation to ours. If we overlook that, we'll surely miss out on the beneficial life lessons they have to teach us and the fulfillment these lessons—and the animals themselves—can bring.

Through my experience with Jiggs, I was able to access my true passion and deeper purpose, fulfilling my mission here on Earth. I'm not sure what my life would have looked like had I ignored the nudgings from Jiggs or not acted on them, but I do know that changing the entire direction of my life has brought me a much deeper joy and a greater sense of purpose than I'd ever imagined. Discovering my healing gifts opened me up to an entirely new world that I've been privileged to share with many others.

Having experienced my own transformation, I can say definitively that life requires embracing the new at times and being open to change. And if the way is shown to us through an animal companion, it's for an important reason and shouldn't be ignored.

## Reflections

Reflect on a time in your life when you used your intuition and inner knowing and discovered your best guidance and path.

1. Have you ever not trusted your instincts regarding what's best for an animal companion?
2. Has an animal ever helped you follow your intuition or gut feeling?
3. What happened, and what did you learn?

## Exercise: Tuning In

Animals are teachers, and one of the quickest ways to receive and embody the teachings an animal has for you is to learn to be more in tune with them. One of the first steps in learning to be more in tune with them is mastering the art of quieting the mind to eliminate mental chatter and inner noise. This is one of the most important skills to become proficient in if you want to open yourself to receive teachings from the animals.

I'm sure you've experienced that pesky inner voice that sometimes takes over the otherwise peaceful environment inside your mind. For some of us, this voice can be like an annoying diatribe, reminding us of what we can't possibly do, learn, or master, no matter what new skill we're embarking on. It can be downright negative—it's often called the inner critic or monkey mind. I'm sure most of you can identify with that. For others, this voice may be a dull hum that is just loud enough to keep us from entering the focused, meditative, or contemplative state we need to be in to fully tap into and receive the rich inner gems that are waiting for us.

Understanding that the mental chatter or inner noise we often hear is a form of self-sabotage helps put it into perspective for us. Regardless of what your inner voice sounds like, it is critical to learn to quiet it in order to really focus on using your senses to commune and communicate with the animals. My belief is that we are constantly being sent information from them, but oftentimes we're just too "busy" to receive it—or rather, our minds are just too cluttered to even notice it.

Hearing these tidbits is often easiest for people who practice some form of relaxation technique on a regular basis: meditation, drumming, yoga, or simply walking in nature (without music on, of course). Making a concerted effort to spend time in a quiet environment is also helpful, so be mindful of how much noise enters your world on a regular basis.

Do you always have the TV or radio on? Do you work in a noisy environment? If you must listen to music, try to pick music that feeds and soothes your soul and helps you get into a relaxed state. There is much great music to choose from, and a couple of my favorites are Deva Premal and Jaya Lakshmi.

I believe that each of you has already been sent important messages from your animal companions, even those on the other side, but many of you may not have been quiet enough to "receive" them properly. They'll be so excited when your mind is quiet enough to start to take note!

When we've mastered being quiet on the inside, as I like to call it, we can "listen to" and hear all living beings. That might feel like a stretch for some, but trust me—it's true!

The following exercise can be done as a visualization or meditation—or, if you don't feel confident that you can do either of those options, simply go through the exercise and pretend or act as if you are doing it (you will still receive benefits from doing it this way).

1. Prepare a space as free from noise and distraction as possible where you can relax, undisturbed.

2. To begin, uncross your arms and legs, straighten your back, and bring yourself into a relaxed and comfortable position—either sitting or lying down.

3. Take a couple of deep, cleansing breaths, inhaling through the nose and exhaling through the mouth. As you breathe in, visualize breathing in universal white light healing energy and exhaling any cares, worries, fears, or doubts you may have.

4. Ground yourself as we did in the exercise in chapter 3.

5. Now that you're in a focused state, strongly declare to or command the universe and your higher self (the highest spiritual expression of you) that you release any thoughts or mind chatter that may block your ability to receive communication from the animals. This is very powerful! Below are a couple of examples of declarations you can say, but be sure to use wording that you resonate with: *I now create a quiet environment within for the purposes of listening to and hearing the message the animals have to share with me. So be it. Quiet, quiet, quiet; I now command focus and attention and release any unbeneficial mental thoughts and chatter!*

6. Notice how you feel after this—physically, emotionally, and mentally.

7. Set a strong intention that simply by doing this exercise, you are setting the stage to be more in tune with your animal companion.

8. Be assured that you can come back to this space often by simply visualizing this feeling and time.

9. Feel gratitude for this process.

10. Feel your feet on the floor, take a couple of conscious breaths, and come back to present awareness.

I encourage you to revisit this exercise often via whichever method you chose; later, you can branch out and experiment with some of the other methods.

# Chapter 5

# Learning About Life and Leadership

*Teaching is leaving a vestige of oneself in the development of another. And surely the student is a bank where you can deposit your most precious treasures.*

~EUGENE P. BERTIN

"I lost a dear friend on the winter solstice of 2013," writes Lenore. "His name was Oscar, a handsome elderly burro. But though he has passed, I will never forget the lessons he taught me."

Oscar had come into Lenore's life in the summer of 2010, and as is often the way with our animal companions, she had no idea at the time how profoundly he would come to influence her life. Having visited a burro rescue in Southern Arizona, Lenore knew she had to adopt him after the two had formed an instant bond.

A few years later, Lenore finally fulfilled her dream of finding a place of her own in the country, moving there with Oscar and Henry, a blind burro she'd acquired as a companion for Oscar. There, she could have both sweet boys with her, and despite her trepidations about how the two would get along, Oscar quickly became Henry's guide and protector.

The farm was idyllic, the perfect place for Lenore and her boys: a delightful house, a few acres of pasture, and a well-kept barn. Every morning when she stepped out the door, she counted her blessings as she smelled the clean air, touched the fresh grass, and heard Oscar braying at her to hurry up with their breakfast. It was an ideal, peaceful sanctuary for Lenore and her sweet burros to settle down.

In the first few weeks the two were together, Lenore wasn't sure how Oscar would react to Henry. Despite the years she had spent around burros, Lenore couldn't truly say she understood everything about them—how they think, what they feel. Would Oscar even notice that Henry was blind, for example? Would he like him? Would he look after him? Or—and this was Lenore's greatest fear—would Oscar simply ignore him?

Although most adapt well to vision loss, blind equines require a safe environment and very special management, which Lenore knew and planned for when she agreed to look after Henry. To her surprise, all her fears were laid to rest in the first few days the two burros were together. Oscar took to looking after Henry as though he had been doing it all his life.

For the first few days, Oscar followed Lenore, watching carefully as she led Henry through a muddy area to the pasture. Soon, she noticed that Oscar seemed to know instinctively when Henry might require a nudge or two in and around the barn. Then, on just the third day, he took charge, stepping up like a caring big brother and leading Henry through the mud to the grassy area without a word from Lenore. Lenore felt her heart sing as she watched the two of them together—Oscar leading, Henry following, as though they had been together for years.

Much like a horse, the way a burro adjusts to blindness has everything to do with its personality rather than the disability itself. Lenore had always thought that Henry had an almost saintly personality, and in his dealings with Oscar, his patience and calming demeanor seemed to rub off. Oscar, who previously could be a bit edgy, was noticeably calmer around Henry. Watching the two of them as they moved around the farm together uplifted Lenore spiritually; they were her angels.

Lenore had never felt such calm. The decision to move to the farm was clearly the right one, and the blossoming relationship between the two burros was a delight to watch. Lenore practiced groundwork training with Oscar often, and as they moved around the pasture, Henry would follow them with his head, turning slowly so that he could keep track of where they were.

When they finished and Lenore released Oscar, the first thing he would always do was trot over to Henry, exchange a gentle greeting, and then stand beside him while Henry softly nuzzled his neck.

Through the first winter, their bond grew and grew. As spring bloomed and the sun finally appeared after a week of heavy rain, Lenore was keen to get the boys out into the pasture. She fed them their breakfast, then let them out of their stalls, watching as they trotted happily out toward the pasture.

Suddenly, Oscar slipped on the wet mud, landing heavily on his side. Her heart in her throat, Lenore raced over to him, dropping to her knees in the mud beside him. He was lying on his side, breathing heavily, and Lenore could tell right away that he couldn't get back up by himself. Henry hovered nearby, sensing something was wrong.

Fighting back a wave of tears, Lenore stroked his neck as he looked up at her. "I told him not to give up, and he didn't," Lenore recounts. "I just couldn't let him go that day; I wasn't ready, and perhaps sensing my determination, he fought for me. It took a while, but eventually, with lots of grit and determination and slipping and sliding, we got him back on his feet." Lenore was relieved to get him back upright, but as he moved gingerly around the paddock, she could see that something had changed; he wasn't moving in his usual way. He seemed listless and nervous.

Something went out of Oscar that day, and he remained very weak, so it was no surprise to Lenore when he slipped and fell again a week later, the morning of December 21, 2013. "Of course I raced to him once more, but as soon as I reached him, I could tell that this was the beginning of the end. I didn't even ask him to get up this time," Lenore recalls. "I could see that it wasn't going to happen. He was so still—peaceful, even—so instead of pushing him to get to his feet, I asked him to stay calm, told him that I was with him, and said that the vet was on his way to end his pain and struggles." This senior friend didn't deserve any more suffering.

Henry hovered nearby, pacing nervously, sensing something was wrong even if he couldn't see it. Lenore led him back to the barn, then returned to Oscar. "While we waited," she recalls, "I fed him bits of apples and pears. He always gave great kisses, and at one point, he lifted his head, reached across, and kissed my face. I was so distraught that I could barely breathe, but I kept it together as best as I could for him. I didn't want him to be afraid or stressed in his last moments, so I suppressed my emotions. I put everything I could into making his final moments, his transition, as calm and peaceful as possible."

After Oscar passed, when emotions threatened to take Lenore down, she would hear the song "Everything's Gonna Be Alright" in her head. She also remembered a license plate she saw on the day Oscar moved to the farm that translated to "all will be fine." Both felt like messages from the spirit realm. "I don't think I had ever been open to messages of this sort before," recalls Lenore. "But in the days after Oscar's death, I was so open, so raw, I think all my usual filters were ripped off. Instead of immediately rejecting the possibility that these might be messages to me, I noticed them and took comfort in them."

On Christmas Day, four days after Oscar's passing, Lenore's electricity was off for several hours until late into the night. "I sat quietly, surrounded by the soft light of candles and oil lamps," she remembers. "I was thinking about Oscar and Henry and everything that had transpired. It was a time of meditation and deep healing for me. I had a strong feeling that I was being guided to 'be still and heal.' I knew these were all messages from my boy Oscar."

As Lenore reflected on Oscar and his passing, she began to see the ways in which he had influenced her. His calm and gentle leadership with Henry was something that she felt she could take into her everyday life—as well as his delight at the little moments in daily life, from enjoying his breakfast to galloping around the pasture for the sheer, unadulterated joy of it.

"When I would lead Henry through the mud to a grassy area and Oscar would follow, Oscar was modeling the calm leadership skills I most needed to develop. He also taught me to ask for help, which I've never been good about doing. I know that my sweet angel is watching over all of us," she adds. "Oscar's presence here is strong, blessing us all and surrounding us in love."

While Lenore knows that Oscar is free of pain and running with the spirit burros in the sky, it is the memories of what he taught her—and Henry, too—that are his legacy, the eternal gift that will never die. The faith that blind Henry learned in following Oscar, listening to the bell Lenore had put on Oscar, could be Oscar's crowning achievement. For Henry's remaining years, not a day went by without Lenore talking to Henry about Oscar. It felt completely natural, and it seemed to comfort them both.

Although Lenore knew she could never replace Oscar, she also knew that Henry needed a companion. So, just a few short weeks after Oscar's passing, Henry was joined by Cash, a beautiful red roan rescue burro with a calm, steady personality.

Cash quickly took on Oscar's role of looking after Henry, which was yet another surprise for Lenore. Burros can often be territorial and can take a while to get used to new situations and companions, so Lenore was relieved when Cash fit right in. To Lenore, it seemed as though Oscar was always there in spirit, leading, teaching, and helping Cash adapt to his new role. And although Henry quickly came to love and trust Cash, he still came and found Lenore every day to spend their special time together talking about Oscar.

Oscar was buried with an apple and a pear, which were always good for a kiss, and some carrots, along with an amethyst for protection and to enhance spirit connection. Not long after, Lenore witnessed an extraordinary sight that sent tingles running down her spine. As she walked out into the pasture leading Henry, Lenore noticed some neighboring horses and mules clearly standing over Oscar's grave, as though paying their respects. She stood very still, just watching them as they stood sentry over the grave for quite some time. One in particular, who looked a lot like Oscar, had really bonded with him over the gate, and long after the other animals had wandered away, he stood in silent vigil over Oscar's grave. Seeing the visit and their silent ceremony gave Lenore an extraordinary feeling of peace and well-being. She knew they would most likely have occasional sightings of Oscar's spirit when he returned for earthly visits and was sure they could still communicate with him the way animals do with those who have departed.

Despite her awareness that Oscar is still with her on some level, Lenore still misses his sweet brays when she walks out the door, his silhouette at the entrance to the barn, his patient escort around the yard, and even his stink eye when she was too slow getting out for breakfast.

We can experience truly profound connections with burros or any animal, even when they have passed into the spiritual realm. When Lenore describes how Oscar continues to lead her in the years following his passing, it very much mirrors my experience with Lucero (see chapter 7), one of the most profound and powerful animal relationships that I have ever experienced.

"I believe that my relationships with Oscar, Henry, and Cash were and are very *real*, very personal, and very important in what they taught me and continue to teach me about behavior and leadership," says Lenore. What we learn from animals may be even more significant than any of us realize, and it can have important real-world applications.

Everyone is a leader in some aspect of their lives. While a leader can often behave like someone to simply be obeyed (and many people enjoy taking on this type of position in some area), the most effective leadership requires partnership and more of a soft-spoken style. Sometimes just a calm reassurance or a gentle nudge is all that is required, similar to the way Oscar led Henry. These can be important principles to remember when dealing with animals and humans alike. Lenore learned that in any relationship or partnership—even with oneself—qualities such as patience, gentleness, and attentiveness are key to accomplishing any goals. Whether that applies to training an animal or leading a group, the guidance we receive from animals is invaluable.

Through spending time with animals, we become more grounded and centered and more aware of the interconnectedness of all beings. This helps us further expand and open ourselves to our divine gifts, allowing us to experience firsthand the impact of powerful leadership skills, including clear communication, purpose, trust, respect, and understanding.

## Lesson

While we may not always recognize in the moment that an animal is teaching us about leadership, it's valuable to look back and view what we've learned in hindsight. The teachings an animal offers can be subtle, gentle instructions that lead us down a certain path—or a deliberate reminder to be open to new and unique opportunities. Regardless of the complexity of their teaching, our willingness to be aware of, accept, and utilize the leadership and apply it to our own lives and the lives of others will most certainly bring greater fulfillment and lead us toward our destiny, bringing us closer to becoming the people we were meant to be.

By watching Oscar lead Henry and learning from it, Lenore was able to apply the wisdom she gathered to her own life. Her willingness to communicate and form a connection with her animal friends placed her in the position to receive instruction and guidance, allowing her to grow and to nurture and eventually to lead future animal companions throughout her life. When we do the same, we receive benefits that we are able to pass on to others, fulfilling both our purpose and the purpose of the animals here on Earth.

## Reflections

Reflect on a relationship with an animal that opened you up to a new way of being, thinking, or behaving.

1. Have you ever learned something that felt like a life lesson from an animal companion?
2. How did that look and feel?
3. What changes have you noticed in yourself as a result of that?

## Exercise: Meeting Your Guides and Helpers

Lenore communicated with her burros in multiple ways. One important step in learning to do that for ourselves is learning to work with our guides and helpers.

Each of us has a group of guides and helpers assigned to us. Our guides consist of a group of mostly nonphysical beings, including our ancestors, loved ones who have passed on—both human and animal—and angels, archangels, as well as other beings, sometimes well-known. For example, Edgar Cayce, a prominent American clairvoyant who lived in the late 1800s and early 1900s, or Saint Francis of Assisi, the patron saint of animals who had a great love for all of God's creatures. Basically, any benevolent being can be a guide for you.

Our guides are our own personal support team residing in the spirit realm with the goal of helping us excel in all our endeavors. They are here to help, protect, and support us in all areas of our lives. Some are eagerly waiting to come forth to facilitate and assist us with a specific task, like learning to communicate with animals. Other guides are already helping us, with or without our knowledge.

I refer to our group of guides for animal communication as our healing team. Two of the major players on my healing team are my late golden retriever, Jiggs, whom you met in chapter 4, and the late Andalusian stallion Lucero, whom you will meet in chapter 7. They are both guides and helpers for me in my work and are also very willing to assist my students.

You don't have to know the players on your team individually to receive benefits from them—simply having an awareness of them, trusting and knowing they are there, and acknowledging them is enough to begin your relationship with them. You're going to call in your healing team now—specifically, those who are with you—to help you begin communicating with the animals.

The following exercise can be done as a visualization or meditation—or, if you don't feel confident that you can do either of those options, simply go through the exercise and pretend or act as if you are doing it (you will still receive benefits from doing it this way).

1. Prepare a space as free from noise and distraction as possible where you can relax, undisturbed.

2. To begin, uncross your arms and legs, straighten your back, and bring yourself into a relaxed and comfortable position—either sitting or lying down.

3. Take a couple of deep, cleansing breaths, inhaling through the nose and exhaling through the mouth. As you breathe in, visualize breathing in universal white light healing energy and exhaling any cares, worries, fears, or doubts you may have.

4. Ground yourself as we did in the exercise in chapter 3.

5. Ask my healing team of guides and helpers to come forth to assist you in meeting yours.

6. Now, ask your guides and helpers to come forth to you. Imagine them as a group of benevolent beings, perfectly chosen to assist you with all aspects of ani-

mal communication. You may sense them, see them, or hear them; if not, just trust that they are with you.

7. Ask one of them to identify themselves or show themselves to you.

8. Ask if any of them have a special message for you. Be aware that it may come in the form of words, symbols, colors, feelings, or "knowings."

9. Set a strong intention that simply by doing this exercise, you are one step closer to being more in tune with the animals.

10. Be assured that you can come back to your healing team often by simply visualizing this exercise.

11. Feel gratitude toward your healing team.

12. Feel your feet on the floor, take a couple of conscious breaths, and come back to present awareness.

I encourage you to revisit this exercise often via whichever method you chose to do it; later, branch out and experiment with some of the other methods.

## Chapter 6
# Opening to Intuition

*For to be free is to live in a way*
*that enhances the freedom of others.*
~NELSON MANDELA

The early autumn chill laced the breeze that met Katie on the way out of the barn. Normally, this would be cause for her to stop, breathe deeply, look up at the clear blue sky, and exclaim, "What a perfect day."

But this day was far from perfect. In fact, it was just plain awful. It was all Katie could do to put one foot in front of the other as she made her way up the path to her house to make the phone call—the call she had been dreading for the past six weeks.

Jack, her beautiful, tall, eighteen-year-old bay thoroughbred gelding had been going downhill for months, but Katie had only let herself acknowledge it six weeks before when the veterinarian came out for a routine barn call for shots and deworming for Katie's horses. At the end of the visit, Katie had asked her if she could also take a look at Jack, who had been a little off his feed and seemed to be getting a little "ribby." She hoped against hope this was a case of worms or maybe a bad tooth ... anything but what she somehow felt in her heart was going on with Jack, who appeared to be wasting away before her eyes.

The vet thumped around on Jack, listened to his heart, looked at his eyes and ears and teeth, and ran an ultrasound machine over several areas of Jack's body. As Katie tried to read the expression on the vet's face, she could feel white-hot dread coursing through her body. Finally, Dr. Robinson turned to Katie and said the words that still echoed in Katie's head. "I can't really feel any sort of mass anywhere," Dr. Robinson had said gently. "But I've seen enough of these signs to know that what this poor old guy probably has is some sort of systemic cancer."

Trying to speak around the lump in her throat proved useless, so Katie had just nodded mutely. She knew the doctor was right, and yet her mind still scrambled for hope. As if recognizing this, Dr. Robinson continued. "We could do a bunch of tests to determine exactly what it is and how far advanced," she said, her voice clinical, matter-of-fact. It was much easier this way for both of them. "But you and I both know that whatever it is, given Jack's age and condition, even if you treat it, you're not going to cure it—and you'd be doing nothing more than prolonging his misery."

Katie nodded, her mind trying to process these words while her heart slowly shattered, her stomach twisting itself into tight, painful knots. "You're not asking for my opinion, but if you were— if this were my horse—I'd make the rest of his days as happy as I could and then be ready to let him go when the time comes," Dr. Robinson said, removing her stethoscope, closing up the ultrasound device, and returning them both to her medical bag.

Katie nodded, looking toward her boots and trying unsuccessfully to fight back the tears that now streamed down her cheeks, stinging both her eyes and her skin. "How will I know when it's time?" she mumbled, somehow managing to pull some coherent words from her racing mind, the question somehow strong enough to force its way up through her dread.

"You'll know," Dr. Robinson said, looking from Jack to Katie and back again. "The two of you seem very connected. He'll tell you when he's ready to go."

For the next few weeks, every day since that first awful moment of knowing, Katie spent every possible moment with Jack, mostly just sitting with him in his stall, just being together. These were bittersweet days, filled with tears and treats and long, long talks.

From the day Katie had bought Jack on a last-minute whim at a sale, there had been a very special connection between them. She bought Jack to be a companion horse for her other horses when she was on the road. He was beautiful to look at—and delightful to ride—but she never would have guessed that Jack would turn out to be her "heart horse." Of all the horses she had ever owned, Jack was the one with whom she had shared her deepest secrets, her greatest desires, and her most debilitating insecurities.

Jack saw her, knew her, and in that deep pool of reflection, had urged her toward hope and healing time after time. It seemed that Jack could read not only her mind, but also her mood, knowing how she was feeling from her very first step into the barn or corral. And whatever they did that day, Jack somehow always managed to put Katie right.

*Who will put me right now? What will happen when I no longer have Jack to look out for me?* At the time, she asked the questions of no one in particular.

Eventually, the day did come, and Katie had no doubt that Dr. Robinson was right this time. While Jack pressed against her, his huge head cradled in her arms, he had responded to her question, "Is it time, my Jackie?" with a huge, bone-deep sigh. There was a peace there, Jack seemingly still trying to provide her reassurance, but Katie couldn't help but ask herself the question: *Is it really time?* Her thoughts bounced around inside her head. *Are you sure? How do you know he doesn't have a few more days?* But when the time came, she forced the words out and made the appointment for Dr. Robinson to come out the next morning.

Katie spent that last night with Jack in his stall, curled up with a blanket and crying most of the night. She must have drifted off to sleep, because when she opened her eyes at daybreak, Jack was standing over her, head down close to hers, his warm breath brushing against her bangs. She reached up to touch his soft muzzle, desperate to memorize every last detail. His once-bright eyes were dull and soft upon her, soulful but resigned, as though he knew how much this was hurting her and wanted to take that agony away.

"It's okay, Jackie," she said, feeling a little guilty. *I should be the one comforting him,* she chided herself. *And here he is comforting me.* "I'll be okay, Jack. I'm just going to miss you so … so much." Katie fought back the tears, suddenly self-conscious for adding her grief to his physical pain. "Let's get out in the sunshine for a while, shall we?" she heard herself say, reaching for Jack's halter and slipping it into place for the very last time.

Katie and Jack walked through the corral, stopping for him to touch noses with each of the other horses—even the pony he'd never had any real use for—a solemn, holy experience that Katie couldn't help but marvel at through her tears.

They made their way through the back gate of the arena and to the back field where the grass was tall, green, and lush. Jack sniffed at the fresh green grass and attempted to graze—more for the experience than hunger, it seemed.

The low rumble of Dr. Robinson's truck entering the front gate brought Jack's head up from his feigned grazing. He turned and moved closer to Katie, putting his head against her chest as he always used to do when they'd had a particularly good day. Katie stroked his neck and tried not to think.

Out of the corner of her eye, Katie saw movement across the field. Turning, she saw a huge, magnificent red-tailed hawk land near the midpoint of the telephone wire that stretched across their twelve-acre Vermont farm. As the hawk landed, the wire dipped beneath his weight. Katie wondered absentmindedly if the wire would break. The hawk sat, framed dramatically by the white mountains of New Hampshire in the distance as Dr. Robinson and her two assistants walked across the field toward them. As they approached, Katie wrapped her arms around Jack's beautiful head. "I'll love you forever," she whispered through her tears.

Dr. Robinson stroked Jack's neck. "I know this is incredibly hard, Katie, but you're doing the right thing," she told her. "As guardians of our animals, we have to be prepared for one of the hardest things we'll ever have to do." She paused. "It's also the most loving thing we can do when an animal gets to this place and can't get any better."

She looked at Katie empathetically, then added, "But that doesn't mean it doesn't break our hearts." Katie nodded, releasing her grip on Jack and fishing a soggy Kleenex out of her pocket to dab at her raw and running nose.

"I don't know if you've ever been through this before," Dr. Robinson said gently, "but sometimes a horse will react kind of violently when the euthanasia drug hits his system."

Watching the horror rise in Katie's eyes, she quickly added, "That doesn't mean he's in pain or having a bad experience. It's just a reflex—a body's way of reacting to the drug. The horse really isn't conscious at that point." Dr. Robinson paused. "Most of them don't go that way. We always give them plenty of sedative first, but it can happen. So, after you say goodbye, I'm going to need you to step back a good way to make sure you're safe."

Katie nodded. *As if this couldn't get any worse*, she thought. She cradled Jack's head one last time, looking deeply into his soulful eyes. "Goodbye, Jackie. I love you," she whispered as she gave him a last kiss on his nose and let his soft muzzle deliver a gentle kiss of his own on her neck, just as he had always done. Then she stepped about ten feet away to Jack's right side, to the shady area where Dr. Robinson had gestured. Looking up, Katie saw that she was facing the big red hawk, who was still watching them from the sagging telephone line as if he were supervising.

To avoid putting a picture in her head she could never erase, Katie kept her eyes on the hawk as Dr. Robinson prepared to make the lethal injection. To her surprise, however, just as Dr. Robinson announced to her assistants that she was making the injection, the hawk took flight, rising from the wire and flying straight toward them. At the moment the hawk passed over Jack, the horse leaped high into the air, all four feet off the ground, and then came back down in a crumpled heap on the ground. Dr. Robinson ran over with her stethoscope to confirm what Katie already knew. He was gone.

As if in a slow-motion fog, Katie thanked the vets, accepted the piece of Jack's tail they clipped off and handed to her, and some-how walked all the way across the pasture. She was able to make it back into the house—where her husband, Dan, had waited to give her space in Jack's last minutes—before the dam finally broke. She fell into Dan's arms, her heart broken, but she knew she'd done the right thing, no matter how hard or emotional it was.

The raw sadness gradually began to fade over time, although the ache still hung in her heart. A week later, she was able to talk about it with one of her spiritual facilitator friends, Brenda. When she mentioned the hawk and what had happened, her friend smiled and nodded.

"Is the hawk significant in some way?" Katie wondered, unprepared for the answer.

Her friend smiled. "Oh, yes," she told Katie. "The hawk and the horse have a huge connection. When the hawk flew over and Jack leaped up at that same instant, his soul entered the hawk."

Katie sat still and quiet for a moment, trying to process what Brenda had said. For some strange reason, as weird as it sounded, it made perfect sense to her.

"Jack also wanted you to know that jumping so high in the air was to show you how joyful he was that you had set him free from his pain and suffering, from his old, worn-out body." Without warning, Katie felt the tears returning and flowing freely. She knew deep in her own soul that her friend had put into words something Katie already knew in her heart, even if she hadn't realized it fully. Even Dr. Robinson had been surprised to see how high Jack had leaped, which further confirmed the words of Katie's friend.

When Katie recounted the hawk story to her husband, he became thoughtful. "You know," he told Katie, "I saw that hawk. I just happened to look out the window, and I saw the whole thing." He looked at Katie and smiled. "I can't believe I'm saying this because it sounds so weird, but I think that's exactly what I saw. You set Jack free, and the hawk was there to carry his spirit away."

## Lesson

There isn't an animal person on Earth who doesn't have to make a difficult decision at some point in their lives, and we often find ourselves wishing we could just be pointed in the right direction or given a visible sign in order to avoid making a potential mistake. The fact is, the signs that the animals are showing us are all there, waiting for us if we are receptive to them, and as hard as they may seem, they will always include a gift or silver lining in the end. When we find our hearts being pulled a certain direction time and time again, it's a good indicator to pay attention to what's being communicated to us. No matter the choice we are facing, heeding the advice and divine wisdom of our animal companions can only be beneficial for our lives and theirs, even if it's a tough decision they are guiding us to follow through on.

When faced with her tough decision, Katie was able to pay attention to the signs and trust her intuition. As she became more receptive to animal communication, she recognized that deeper connection not only between herself and her animal companion, but between other animals and with nature as well. Katie trusted the wisdom of her animal companion to let her know when the time was right for him to move on, and it was confirmed even in his passing.

Clearly, animals have spirits just as humans do, and they want us to be aware that they live on, even when their physical bodies don't. Despite the fact that their passing is incredibly difficult for us while we're on this side, we can take comfort in knowing that they're still with us and living on in spirit, just as Katie learned.

## Reflections

Reflect on a relationship with an animal companion where you had to trust your gut to make decisions and choices that were in their best interest.

1. Has an animal companion ever communicated a specific need that forced you to make a hard choice based on that information?
2. What did that look or feel like?
3. In retrospect, do you feel your choice honored your animal's wishes?

## Exercise: Discovering Your Spirit Animal

Now that you've met your guides and helpers in the exercise in chapter 5, it's time to meet another player in your journey to learn to communicate with the animals: your spirit animal. Your spirit animal is another being that can help guide (or further) you in opening and developing your animal communication and healing journey. All sentient beings are equal and have divine wisdom and gifts to share with humanity. Your spirit animal can be any animal—for example, a hawk, bear, or frog—that has a special affinity for you and archetypal traits, gifts, characteristics, meaningful messages, and distinctive beneficial energy to share with you. Once you have discovered your spirit animal, you can call upon or invoke it at any time to infuse your energy field with its special essence.

Spirit animals come to us for various undertakings; they can come to you for different reasons, seasons, or even throughout your entire lifetime. Your spirit animal for animal communication is your lifelong partner that is here to help you specifically learn to communicate with the animals. That doesn't mean you don't currently have other spirit animals, or that others won't join you over time, but for animal communication, your spirit animal has the most to teach you at this time and wants to be part of your process as you work through these exercises.

To learn more about your spirit animal and gain insight into how they can help you develop your gifts, I suggest studying the characteristics, habits, and behaviors of your spirit animal as well as details of their habitat, their breeding practices and offspring, their vocalizations (if any), and basically anything else you can learn about them. All details you glean will provide valuable insights into them. Let's meet your spirit animal!

The following exercise can be done as a visualization or meditation—or, if you don't feel confident that you can do either of those options, simply go through the exercise and pretend or act as if you are doing it (you will still receive benefits from doing it this way).

1. Prepare a space as free from noise and distraction as possible where you can relax, undisturbed.

2. To begin, uncross your arms and legs, straighten your back, and bring yourself into a relaxed and comfortable position—either sitting or lying down.

3. Take a couple of deep, cleansing breaths, inhaling through the nose and exhaling through the mouth. As you breathe in, visualize breathing in universal white light healing energy and exhaling any cares, worries, fears, or doubts you may have.

4. Ground yourself as we did in the exercise in chapter 3.

5. Now, take a moment and bring your awareness to the nature kingdom, since it's much easier to connect with the animal kingdom and all the species of Mother Earth from this place.

6. Give yourself a moment, and place yourself now in the most exquisite natural setting you currently know, or create an idyllic one in your imagination.

7. See yourself basking in the beauty and serenity of this space and take note of its characteristics.

8. Now, on the count of three, ask that your spirit animal reveal itself to you, and trust and intend that it does. It could be a four-legged, winged, or finned being. It could even be a reptile or insect. Remember, all beings are equal and have equally relevant divine wisdom to share with you.

9. One, two, three. Voila!

10. Simply visualize/intend/know that your spirit animal is now with you.

11. Which animal has come forth for you? Your spirit animal's presence may be fleeting, like a flash, or they may stick around for a while. Either way, you now have your spirit animal for the purposes of this work.

12. Be assured that you can come back to this space often to connect with your spirit animal simply by visualizing this feeling and time.

13. Feel gratitude for your spirit animal.

14. Feel your feet on the floor, take a couple of conscious breaths, and come back to present awareness.

I encourage you to revisit this exercise often via whichever method you chose to do it and to branch out and experiment with some of the other methods.

section three
# Animal Companion as Guide

# Chapter 7

# Receiving Transformational Breakthroughs

*A great horse will change your life.*
*The truly special ones define it.*
~AUTHOR UNKNOWN

After my enlightening course in the barn at Stratford, Ontario, the instructor had mentioned that Lucero, the horse I had spoken with, lived nearby in Newmarket, Ontario. I was thrilled when she suggested that I might like to meet him in person. My experience communicating with Lucero just through a photograph had been so profound that I was truly excited at the prospect of communicating with him face-to-face.

I contacted the owner, and we arranged a meeting for the next week. I have to confess, I counted down the days like a kid waiting for Christmas, and on the short drive out to the farm, I was nervous, wondering what the experience would be like. I was excited at the thought of a deep, profound connection, and I was also concerned that it might not live up to my expectations.

The farm was at the end of a long driveway, hidden behind an old stand of sturdy oak trees. As I pulled up in front of the house, the owner, Mr. Walters, appeared from the back of the property, a smile on his face. "I was in the barn, out back," he told me. "I didn't see you pull up, but Lucero let me know you'd arrived."

Mr. Walters walked me back to the barn to meet Lucero formally in person. As we approached Lucero's stall, I could see that he was beautiful beyond words, his magnificent spirit glowing like the halo around the moon on a clear desert night.

I think Mr. Walters could feel my nervous anticipation as I approached Lucero's stall. He stood back and let me spend a moment just gazing at the magnificent steed. Finally, I reached a tentative hand out toward Lucero.

I can only describe that first meeting with Lucero as awe-inspiring. It felt as though the heavens had opened and the energy was flowing into me. My life changed irrevocably in an instant.

Nearly overwhelmed by how clearly and powerfully Lucero spoke to me, my heart began to expand, and I could feel the energy tingling in waves over my body. Being in the presence of a master is profound, a big deal no matter the situation. It was as though I'd been transported from the physical realm to another dimension where language was different—as if our souls became one.

After a few minutes, Mr. Walters offered to take Lucero out of his stall and over to a paddock where we'd be less confined. I watched, enthralled, as he led Lucero out. Lucero was larger than life, magnificent, grand, omniscient, displaying inner and outer strength. He was also spirited, as would be expected from such a vibrant stallion.

As I mentioned in chapter 4, Lucero was an Andalusian, a breed known for their bold personalities and adventurous spirit. They are fearless, intelligent and sensitive, natural performers, and highly adaptable to different circumstances. And did I mention spirited? Lucero was all of the above and more!

When I met Lucero, it was as though a huge piece of the spiritual puzzle that was my life had been fulfilled. As I stood in the pasture beside him, the sun on my back and the cool, fresh grass beneath my feet, he let me know he'd been with me since long before this meeting, guiding me toward my destiny.

It was beyond wonderful to actually meet such a powerful ally. William Shakespeare described Andalusians almost perfectly when he wrote in *Henry V,* "He is pure air and fire; and the dull elements of earth and water never appear in him, but only in patient stillness while his rider mounts him; he is indeed a horse, and all other jades you may call beasts." [2]

After my first meeting with Lucero, he volunteered through telepathic communication to continue channeling information to me moving forward, giving me concrete directives for my life and business. He offered a clear picture of the logo I was to use in my business and encouraged me to seek deeper training in this brand-new genre I was stepping into. This is one of the most profound connections I've ever had with an animal, and I have never been the same since that encounter. Although Lucero has since passed, he remains one of my spirit guides whom I lovingly refer to as an ascended master of the equine realm.

Once we had met physically, messages from Lucero began to pour into me, as if a dam had broken. Initially, receiving information from him felt like drinking from a fire hose—it was not possible to get it all down on paper or even to share it verbally with others at the rate it was coming in. It was as if someone was talking to me at five times the speed of a normal conversation,

---

2. William Shakespeare, *Henry V* (London: Gardner, 1910), 3.7.21–25.

and all I could do was grab at bits and pieces of this exquisite and profound dialogue as it washed over me. It took me time to learn to "transcode" Lucero's messages. They came in various forms—not just words, but feelings, impressions, pictures, symbols, certainties, and sometimes even just feelings of "knowing" but not knowing *how* I knew. I soon realized that I had always received the information he was transmitting to me, but I was only now becoming aware of the fact that it was coming from him. He told me that animals have divine wisdom and healing to share with humanity. That is one of the greatest reasons they have partnered with us; they see it as their mission. He let me know that my role is to help spread his message.

On one occasion in Arizona, I received a clear communication from Lucero that I should visit a specific beach—"dog beach" in Santa Barbara, California—to commune with the dolphins. I wasn't sure exactly what to expect, but my experience was nothing short of magical. Each time I traveled to the beach from my hotel, the dolphins appeared, communicating with me, attuning me and up-leveling my energy field. I knew intuitively that they were encouraging me toward more advanced healing in my work; it wasn't something I could put into words, but I sensed it within my soul.

As we talked, I felt a deep sense of expansiveness in my body and a surge of energy in each of my chakras, opening me to the dolphins' higher wisdom. Lucero had told me it was important that I commune with the dolphins in person, that they wanted to initiate a connection with me so that I could be a conduit, a portal through which they could transmit information, allowing me to communicate further with other animals. The dolphins wanted to "initiate" me, and as if to prove it, they left a mark on me—literally. I noticed when getting ready that morning that I had a mark near my solar plexus; not paying it too much attention, I went on with my day. However, I noticed that the more time went on, the darker it got—as if I'd gotten a tan only in that small area—and it was in the perfect shape of a dolphin! This synchronicity was too much to ignore, and I began showing a few people over the next several days and weeks, one of whom said, "You've been marked by the dolphins for communication."

This profound experience illustrates the interconnectedness of all beings. Lucero knew that I needed to be in the physical presence of the dolphins for the next progression of my spiritual journey, and it was he who set that in motion. His instructions never fail me.

There were no further rock-my-world moments in our relationship, but rather just a steady flow of information, guidance, and knowledge. It felt as though we were merged as one, and the information and guidance eventually began to come in as gently and naturally as my own thoughts, with the feeling of "drinking from a fire hose" gradually falling away over time.

The presence of Lucero's spirit, both when he was alive on this earthly plane and after he crossed over, is like a golden thread that is woven through every element of my life and every fiber of my being. Everything I've done since I connected with him has been informed by and guided by his being, with the process only intensifying over time. Looking back, I can now see his influence in so many turning points and crucial decisions in my life, in the moments that have accumulated to form the person I am today. One example is when, with Lucero's direction, I decided to sell my house in Toronto, leaving behind my entire life as I knew it to create a brand-new one in Sedona, Arizona. I visited first a couple of times and eventually got a business visa so I could reside in the mystical hub. At the time, I was a realtor, and while

I was successful, the career was no longer fulfilling on a soul level for me.

Another example—changing the direction of my own business toward coaching individuals in theirs to incorporate proven business principles with their divine gifts and intuitive abilities—led to much more satisfaction and deep soul fulfillment. Later, being guided by Lucero to circle back to my animal communication and healing business—now focused primarily on teaching others—resulted in my greatest success, thanks to his transformative guidance and wisdom.

With Lucero beside me, my knowledge and understanding of the invisible realm began growing exponentially, and the same can be true for any of us. Once we quiet our minds, open our hearts, and connect with the energies of the earth, animals will reach out to connect with us or be open to us initiating connection with them. They can help us communicate not only with themselves, but with other animals. They can help us learn to heal—both ourselves and others—and will offer to stand alongside us as powerful guides, helping us with our own lives and helping us help others.

Lucero has traversed time with me on this journey, and I carry with me his wisdom. While this work is spiritual in nature, Lucero encourages us to remain easygoing and lighthearted about it. "Be as easy as my warm breath flowing into your heart chakra," Lucero has said. "Don't be too serious; be loose and natural, like water flowing over river rocks. Be open, and you will receive."

One night, soon after I'd moved to Sedona, Lucero's spirit woke me up in the middle of the night, demanding that I get out of bed to receive an important "download" from him. I was sleepy, snuggled up warm under the covers, and the last thing I wanted to do was get up. However, Lucero was insistent and said this couldn't wait until morning, that the time and energy were perfect at that moment.

As I crawled reluctantly out of bed and pulled on my robe, he gave me very explicit instructions directing me to get pen and paper and sketch a horse's body. Once I had done that, Lucero began to guide me to mark various points on the body that he said were at the intersections of grid lines of energy. He told me that they were portals to deeper healing and urged me to play around with them and incorporate them into my healing work, which of course I did.

**Lucero's Portal Points**

Once I began using Lucero's suggested portal points (which you will be able to incorporate in a later exercise) in my animal healing sessions with clients, many of them reported that their animal companions were healing rapidly, with behavioral issues dissipating and health concerns resolving. Some clients even reported that the health concerns their animals experienced—even those thought to be incurable—had mysteriously resolved, to the surprise of their veterinarians.

"[Lucero] came to me from behind and softly breathed in my ear," Stephanie, one student, told me. "It opened all my intuitive channels at once. I could feel him, smell him, and hear him. He filled me with confidence; it wasn't until after we spent a few minutes in the presence of each other in a meditative state that he walked in front of me. After I took in his beauty, he invited me to follow him, walking in his confidence."

Another student, Lucy, echoes a point that I have always felt about Lucero—there is no artifice in him, and he gives you the unvarnished truth. "Lucero has always been no-nonsense with me and always cuts to the truth," says Lucy. "Metaphorically, when he stamps his hooves, time stops and you listen. I love him and have a deep respect for all that he has shared with me. He has taught me to stop being afraid and to run toward my dreams."

Even students who have never met him in person or seen pictures of him describe him accurately. After one of my workshops, a woman named Delia told me, "In my mind's eye, Lucero stepped in front of me in all his glory, glowing, with his mane blowing in the wind. He was just glorious. He told me to own my power and my gift and not to play small. He said I'm not currently utilizing my gifts to the best of my ability. I loved my experience with him; he is so wise and caring."

## Lesson

As we see, animals can be extraordinary guides in more ways than one. From the subtle to the prominent, their guidance is displayed to help us become our truest selves, use our unique gifts, and realize our divine calling. Whether it's a horse as majestic and powerful as Lucero or a tiny kitten, each animal has wisdom to share.

We have many levels of guides. For the most part, they are helpers, healers, and directors; when they see us veering off track, they can turn into head-scratchers. They are also trusted allies and protectors of our best interests. They are the guardians or gatekeepers of our "divine missions," constantly nudging us in the direction of the highest version of ourselves, encouraging us to express what our souls truly came here to do.

For me, Lucero is the highest-level guide, an exalted being, participating in his own way in everything I do, encouraging me and having a hand in all I create. Initially, he did this from the earthly plane while still in a physical body, but now, since his passing in 2002, he does it from the spirit realm. Once I opened myself to Lucero's guidance, it was as if I opened myself to another world. I began to realize not only how much information he holds, but how much he is willing to share with me when I am receptive. When we recognize the messages and teachings for what they are, we will be guided to a higher level of living, transformed into the beings that the universe intended us to be.

## Reflections

Reflect on a time you feel you have had a transformative relationship with an animal who offered guidance and influenced your life.

1. Have you ever had an experience with an animal that fascinated you and left you awestruck?
2. What was the significance of that interaction?
3. In retrospect, do you feel you received guidance from them?

## Exercise: Opening to Guidance

Opening to the guidance of our animal companions requires having a fully open heart. The connection we strive for is a heart connection with them—their heart to ours. In order to receive information they send us, it is essential that we approach them with an open, unblocked heart.

To have truly open hearts, like those of our animal friends, it is important that we do our own healing work. It's vitally important for us to heal and let go of any unresolved issues that may reside within, whether physical, emotional, mental, or spiritual. This prepares us by allowing for the release of any judgments, belief systems, or imbalances within us that might cloud or interfere with our connection.

In doing this exercise, you will repeat the grounding and quieting the mind pieces from previous exercises, as each of them builds on the other.

1. Prepare a space as free from noise and distraction as possible where you can relax, undisturbed.

2. Uncross your arms and legs, straighten your back, and bring yourself into a relaxed and comfortable position—either sitting or lying down.

3. Take a couple of deep, cleansing breaths, inhaling through your nose and exhaling through your mouth. As you breathe in, visualize breathing in universal white light healing energy and exhaling any cares, worries, fears, or doubts you may have.

4. Now, visualize a beam of white light coming down from above, toward the top of your head (the location

of your crown chakra). Visualize it entering there, slowly coming down through your body, and filling up every cell within you with this white light.

5. Then, visualize the light exiting from the soles of your feet and the base of your tailbone.

6. Visualize the light going down through the floor and any floors below you, connecting you and your energy deep within Mother Earth.

7. Now, bring your attention to your heart center (or heart chakra). Picture two small "French doors," roughly five to six inches in height, in the area of your heart chakra. These are doors that you can open at will.

8. Now, picture opening them outward in a way similar to opening the doors or windows in your home on a warm, sunny day. Experience the feeling of basking in the warm air and bright sunlight that come in, feeling great gratitude for this opening.

9. Consciously visualize and intend that your heart will be open to any information, in any form, that may come your way for the highest benefit of yourself, your animal companions, and all concerned.

10. Set a strong intention that simply by doing this exercise, your heart is now wide open and receptive to your animal companions' guidance.

11. Notice the way you feel in this moment—physically, emotionally, and mentally.

12. If you have an animal companion nearby, notice how they react to you or seem to feel about you when

you're grounded, focused, and have your heart wide open and receptive to them.

13. Be assured that you can come back to this space often by simply visualizing this feeling and time.

14. Feel gratitude for this process.

15. Feel your feet on the floor, take a couple of conscious breaths, and come back to present awareness.

I encourage you to revisit this exercise often via whichever method you chose to do it, and then branch out and experiment with some of the other methods. Again, if you don't feel you're good at visualizing, don't despair; you can accomplish the above, including what I taught in the previous exercises, by simply pretending or imagining that you're doing it. That might sound strange to you, but it's a powerful way into successful visualization for those of you who don't feel you can vizualize.

## Chapter 8
# An Unconventional Guide

*And how she looked at me like I could save her*
*from everything bad in the world. This was my secret:*
*she was the one who saved me.*
~LAUREN OLIVER

Nancy's daughter, Colleen, had just been diagnosed with stage four cancer, which the doctors said had already entered her lymph nodes. Colleen and her seven-year-old cat, Artemis—a beautiful but feisty tortoiseshell who was her companion and sidekick—had just moved into a new place. The cancer diagnosis came right on the heels of a marital separation, so the two of them were going through a deeply traumatic season of life.

Colleen was known for rescuing cats and kittens that were unwanted by others. She had grown quite close to Artemis despite the fact that she was no warm and fuzzy kitty. As Nancy cared for Colleen during her illness, watching her cope with the pain, she did her best to get to know Artemis, who definitely was not what she would call friendly. But she knew that Colleen had a special place in her heart for the kitty, so she tried to tolerate and maybe even befriend her while suffering along with her daughter.

When Colleen passed away, Nancy took Artemis in. She wasn't even sure she wanted to, but she felt that she owed it to Colleen; it was all she had left of her daughter, and she wanted to hold on to anything she could. After all, she didn't know whether she'd be able to find someone who would want Artemis, and she couldn't bear the thought of what might happen to her even if she did.

After taking Artemis home, Nancy realized just how feral the cat truly was; the moves, abuse, traumas, and loss of Colleen had created massive insecurity for this kitty. Not surprisingly, Artemis had been sensing and feeling everything that was happening in the family and was reacting to it, and Nancy had a tough time even getting Artemis to allow her to come near. She felt terrible for the cat after all she'd been through and hoped she might calm down a bit.

For the first few weeks, Nancy stayed with her, slept with her, and sang to her, all while still trying to deal with her own grief. But when Nancy stepped in front of Artemis one day and Artemis bit her hard, she knew things couldn't go on like this indefinitely. Nancy spoke to a veterinarian who warned her that Artemis would always be difficult and advised her to consider putting her to sleep. "She will never change," he told her. "She will always be a wild, uncontrollable cat." But as an animal lover, Nancy wouldn't hear of that.

And then, as if the universe could hear her prayers, Nancy discovered my animal communication and energy healing program. "I can't even remember how I found it," says Nancy. "It just seemed to be the right thing at the right time."

As she began to learn, absorb, and practice the program protocols on Artemis, Artemis slowly began to improve. She gradually allowed Nancy to come closer and then began to accept her touch. Eventually, over time, she started coming much closer to Nancy when she was working and even started to sleep near Nancy's bed. As Artemis's behavior changed, Nancy began to relax and feel like they might just have a chance at becoming friends after all.

Nancy's initial focus with Artemis was on healing and energy clearing; she wasn't ready to try her hand at animal communication yet. It was a very rough time in Nancy's life. She had a great deal of stress and grief to process; she'd lost her beautiful daughter, taken on an equally grieving and unruly cat, and was helping another close family member deal with cancer as well. These were trying times.

However, after a few months, Nancy felt ready to delve deeper into the animal communication component of her training; she committed fully, and over time it became clear that she and Artemis were healing each other at the same time. The idea that this traumatized cat was healing her was deep and profound for Nancy, a revelation that opened her mind to the reality of her situation. It was hard for her to fathom that this cat, who had been through so much and needed so much from her, could at the same time be offering her the very help she needed.

I have found that many people who become interested in learning animal communication and healing are either about to lose an animal companion or have recently lost one. I truly believe their animals guide them to this as a way of helping them both—the same can be said for losing a human. The animals in our lives guide us this way as they understand our own need for deep healing, and they know that when we embark on connecting deeply with another, especially an animal, we are healed in the process.

It was not a quick or easy process for Nancy, trying to integrate Artemis into her family of existing cats—Odin and Diana—but over time, they have all figured out how to navigate day-to-day life together. "Artemis has even learned how to play with other cats," reveals Nancy, "a first for her." She now comes out and spends time with the whole family in the evenings, allowing Nancy to pet her and brush her every night.

They've been together two and a half years now, in which time Nancy has not only completed her training but is now a successful practicing healer. She is convinced that this has been her purpose for a long time and that Artemis has helped her fulfill it. "It's like a little miracle," says Nancy. "Through Artemis, I feel like I still have a living part of my daughter Colleen with me," she says, which is comforting.

I've seen countless situations where people set out to help, save, or rescue an animal in need—in whatever way arises—and then end up being saved themselves in the process, as the story of Nancy and Artemis shows. Most often, the people in these situations barely recognize that they themselves needed saving, or that it is even possible an animal in need might be able to do that for them. It's typically not until looking back on the situation later that they realize the truth of the experience and how the animal healed them.

A similar story was told to me by Ellen, another client of mine, who came to me and shared her life-changing experience. Having always loved cats, Ellen was eager to tell the story of how a beloved feline protected her and guided her to safety.

When a neighbor's cat had a litter of seven kittens, Ellen and her father were keen to adopt one. The two shared an apartment and enjoyed each other's company, but they felt they were ready to bring a new kitten into the family. They had recently lost their beloved Samuel after thirteen happy years together and were desperately missing having a cat around the apartment; the place felt way too empty.

Ellen was excited as they entered the neighbor's apartment. As soon as she stepped inside, she could hear the kittens meowing from across the room. Feeling a tingle of butterflies in her stomach, they crossed the room and looked into the large cardboard box. The chance to add another young life to their family thrilled her.

As Ellen looked down into the box, what she saw looked like a writhing ball of fur. The tiny kittens, wriggling and squirming, peered up at them, their little pink mouths open as they meowed softly. Ellen gazed at them: seven tiny lives, all in need of a good home. Ellen knew that they could provide a good home for any of them, but how could she possibly choose one over the others?

She tried to focus on them one at a time, but every time she fixed her gaze on one of them, a littermate would clamber on top, demanding their turn in the spotlight.

"They're sweet, aren't they?" said her neighbor. "I've got some more folks coming by later to have a look at them, but I knew you'd just lost your old fella not too long ago. Figured you'd like first pick of the litter."

"Thanks," said Ellen, her eyes still trying to separate one kitten from the next. She was starting to feel stressed by the whole thing. She was sure it was going to be too hard to pick one.

Her father sat behind her, watching the cats, then looking up at Ellen. He could sense the difficulty she was having making a choice. "What do you think?" he asked finally. "Do you have a favorite?"

Ellen peered at the kittens again. She could happily take any one of them home with her. "I don't know," she muttered, glancing at her dad. "What about you? Any of them stand out for you?"

Her father peered at the teeny kittens. "That's the one," he said suddenly. His hand darted into the box and plucked out one of the kittens, holding it up for Ellen to see. The little cat blinked at her, meowing softly.

Ellen smiled, looking at her dad. "He's cute," she said, "but why him?"

"He looks like Humphrey Bogart." Her dad laughed.

"And so he did," says Ellen. "So that's what we named him, and he was a special kitty from the very start. I always called him our 'celebrity kitty.'"

Her dad handed Bogart to Ellen and she carried him into their apartment, setting him down on the carpet. Bogart stood still for a moment, taking everything in, then set off to explore the place, still skittish on his thin legs. After a few minutes, he scurried back to Ellen, who was sitting on the floor watching him; he climbed up in her lap and was soon fast asleep.

Bogart quickly settled into his new home amid Ellen's other collection of pets—the parrots and rabbits and even a tank of tropical fish. Like any young kitten, he was interested in all of them and would sit and stare for hours at the fish, but he never tried to get to them.

For a young kitten, Bogart was a peaceful soul. He had his routine, knew when it was dinnertime, knew when Ellen's dad was due home from work. Other than that, he was happy lying in the sun, cuddling up in Ellen's lap, or gazing at the fish. So, when he became restless one night, Ellen took notice.

"That night, Bogart kept pacing back and forth between the kitchen and living room, back and forth, back and forth, just staring at me," Ellen remembers. "At first, I thought he wanted food, but he had already eaten." The kitchen in Ellen's apartment had two entrances, and Bogart just kept circling through and coming back around to stare at her, then looking back toward the kitchen before starting another circle.

Ellen was watching TV, in the middle of her favorite show, snuggled up warm under a blanket. The last thing she wanted to do was get up to see what Bogart was fussing about, but eventually she climbed up off the sofa and followed Bogart into the kitchen, expecting to see a mouse or something similar. "Come on, Bogart," she told him, "show me what's got you so riled up this evening. What's going on, buddy?"

But rather than finding a mouse on the floor, Ellen was greeted by the overpowering smell of gas. One of the pilot lights on the stove was turned on with no flame, and the gas was filling the room. If Bogart hadn't alerted Ellen to the danger, she could have been overcome by fumes or an explosion could have occurred. Bogart's persistence had most likely saved her life, and perhaps those of the other residents, too.

Ellen called her dad, who quickly turned off the gas at the main as she opened all the windows to clear the room. Nearby, Bogart sat and watched the entire time, supervising the situation. When it was all over, the intuitive kitty got an extra treat to eat that night!

In another unprecedented instance, he alerted her to a fire in the building, saving her life yet again. These are not isolated incidents. While Ellen and Bogart are unusual because he has twice alerted her to danger, this is far from the only case I have heard of an animal warning their owners. A quick online search reveals dozens of stories of animals—particularly cats and dogs—alerting their families to danger, mainly fires and gas leaks. Whether it is by barking or meowing, pacing or scratching, even tugging or nipping at their owners, our animal companions find a way to communicate important things to us.

Animals live in the here and now and are highly attuned to what is going on around them. They also take their responsibility for their human family very seriously. This is why it is imperative to pay attention when our animal friends seem to be trying to communicate something to us; after all, it could very well save our lives! My belief is that there is a mutually symbiotic relationship between the discovery and expression of our own missions and the manifestation of the missions of our animal friends who come to help us, which is revealed in the stories of Nancy and Artemis and Ellen and Bogart. While we may suspect we are helping an animal by rescuing or adopting and taking care of them, if we look closer, we will undoubtedly see that it is they who are helping and taking care of us.

## Lesson

There is no shortage of incredible stories of animals alerting people to danger, and it's undeniable that their instincts are sharp and their intuitions strong. But there are so many other ways animals save humans—physically, emotionally, mentally, and spiritually. Animals have a keen sense and are attuned to what we are experiencing—and they know what we need, whether that is to get out of the house quickly or to allow them to heal our broken hearts. In fact, the intuitive and healing gifts of animals are so much more than meets the eye—but we must open ourselves up to not only recognizing and accepting these gifts, but allowing the healing to take place in ourselves.

This doesn't mean we should discount our own gifts and healing abilities, either. In fact, it's very important to recognize these abilities in ourselves in order to see them in other people as well as in animals. Tuning our consciousness to the awareness of subtle communication, both physical and through spiritual means, opens us up to many possibilities we may have otherwise overlooked. This is when mutual healing can occur, just like with Nancy and Artemis, Ellen and Bogart—both cases where the women ended up receiving deep healing in their own lives and souls. As we learn to recognize the deeper purpose or role of an animal companion and develop a relationship of mutual trust, we can strengthen our connection and open the channel for healing to flow in both directions as we are guided by them.

## Reflections

Reflect on a time when an animal guided you to physical safety or mended your shattered heart.

1. Think back on a time when an animal companion nurtured your grief or despair.
2. Have you ever felt like an animal companion was trying to warn you of risk or danger?
3. How did you respond to their guidance—and what was the result?

## Exercise: Balancing Your Chakras

As Nancy learned, one of the program protocols I teach in my training is clearing and balancing your chakras. I introduced chakras in the exercise in chapter 3. As a refresher, chakras are energy portals located in various positions throughout our bodies and are the vehicles through which we receive and assimilate vital universal life force energy. For those who can see energy, they look like spinning cones, with the point located at the spine.

Our chakras have both a front and a back, with one cone opening out in front of the body from the spine and the back of that chakra opening out behind us from the spine.

Each chakra is associated with a specific area of the body and governs the function of nearby bodily components, including organs, bones, skin, blood, tissues, and so on. In addition to relating to our physical bodies, chakras also affect our emotional, mental, and spiritual states of consciousness. Therefore, an imbalance in one of your chakras could impact you on many levels, including your mindset, feeling safe and supported in the world, your ability to feel grounded, your creativity, or your personal power, just to name a few.

Our energy fields are in a constant state of flux, and each chakra is impacted by your day-to-day goings-on and your other chakras. Therefore, a blockage or imbalance in one of your chakras can have a direct impact on the symbiosis of your chakra system as a whole. Because they impact you on multiple levels of consciousness, your chakras play an important role when it comes to actualizing and embodying your animal communication and healing gifts. To learn to connect and align with the animals on the deepest level, it's important to clear, balance, and maintain your chakras at their highest state.

Your seven main chakras are as follows: the root chakra, located at the base of the spine; the sacral chakra, located in the lower abdomen below the navel; the solar plexus chakra, located just below the rib cage; the heart chakra, located at the center of the chest; the throat chakra, located at the throat; the third eye chakra, located at the center of the brows; and the crown chakra, located at the top of the head. All of them are positioned along your spine or midline.

We're going to balance your chakras now.

The following exercise can be done as a visualization or meditation—or, if you don't feel confident that you can do either of those options, simply go through the exercise and pretend or act as if you are doing it (you will still receive benefits from doing it this way).

1. Prepare a space as free from noise and distraction as possible where you can relax, undisturbed.

2. To begin, uncross your arms and legs, straighten your back, and bring yourself into a relaxed and comfortable position—either sitting or lying down.

3. Take a couple of deep, cleansing breaths, inhaling through your nose and exhaling through your mouth. As you breathe in, visualize breathing in universal white light healing energy and exhaling any cares, worries, fears, or doubts you may have.

4. Now, visualize a beam of white light healing energy coming down from above and entering your crown chakra at the top of your head. As it comes down into your body, it slowly fills every cell of your being with this wonderful healing energy.

5. This beam of white light will make its way down the midline along your spine; as it meets each of your chakras, they illuminate like colored light bulbs.

6. Your crown chakra illuminates violet; your third eye, indigo; your throat, sky blue; your heart, green; your solar plexus, yellow; your sacral, orange; and your root, red.

7. As each chakra illuminates, set your intention and visualize it being cleared of any blockages or imbalances and being brought into perfect balance, spinning appropriately.

8. Now, visualize your chakra system as seven illuminated colored lights, all perfectly balanced, energized and ready for you to begin communicating with the animals.

9. Be assured that you can come back to this space often by simply visualizing this feeling and time.

10. Feel gratitude for this process.

11. Feel your feet on the floor, take a couple of conscious breaths, and come back to present awareness.

I encourage you to revisit this exercise often to balance and align your chakras for better access to your animal communication and healing gifts.

# Chapter 9
# Letting Go

*If having a soul means being able to feel love
and loyalty and gratitude, then animals
are better off than a lot of humans.*
~JAMES HERRIOT

"I don't get it," complained Kelly as she gazed out across the perfectly manicured lawn, deep in thought about her horse, Mystic. "I know what Mystic is supposed to be doing, I'm pretty sure he knows what he's supposed to be doing, and Coach Greta trains the Olympic team, so if she doesn't know what she's doing, we're all in trouble." She sighed deeply, lost in her thoughts, the musings mostly rhetorical.

Kelly's husband, Mike, leaned against the breakfast bar silently. After almost twenty-five years together, he knew when to allow Kelly to get her frustrations out and when to step in. *Not yet*, he told himself. *Give her a little more time.*

"There are times when I feel he's almost there," Kelly continued, "then the next day it's back to square one. With the amount of time and money I'm putting in, we should be ready to compete by now, and we're not even close. It's just so frustrating." She slumped down on a barstool, gratefully taking the mug of coffee that Mike slid across to her.

Mike watched her as she slowly sipped her coffee. Little by little, her shoulders started to uncoil, and the lines in her face smoothed out as she began to relax. *Now*—now was the right time. "Perhaps it's time for a different approach," he said softly.

Kelly looked up quickly, surprised by his comment. "I didn't think you—of anyone—would say that."

Mike shrugged. "I'm neutral. But you know what they say about insanity—doing the same thing over and over, expecting different results? I reckon you're ready for a change of pace, something to get you and Mystic out of this rut."

Kelly climbed down from her barstool, wrapped her arms around Mike's neck, and squeezed him tightly. "I knew there was a reason I married you." She laughed. That was when Kelly decided to reach out to me.

It was a couple of weeks before I could get out to Georgia, but I was immediately impressed by Kelly's setup as I looked around the barn. She and Mike lived on the outskirts of Atlanta, in prime horse country—rolling green hills fringed by white wooden fences and dotted with massive barns. Kelly was a financial advisor and had made it clear to me that she would spare no expense in getting things working properly with Mystic, and looking around the barn, I could see that she had the clout to back that statement up. The barn was more luxurious than most people's homes, offering every service, every type of pampering that a horse could need—from dieticians to hydrotherapy, massages to grooming. If Kelly and Mystic were having problems, it certainly wasn't due to a lack of care and attention.

But none of that was important to my work. My work is about connecting with an animal and sharing what I learn from that experience with the client. It can be done in person, but it works equally well over distance. Once I connect with an animal, it doesn't matter where we are; I am able to communicate freely with them. It was only really at Kelly's insistence that I had traveled out to Atlanta, but now that I had done so, I was glad to meet Mystic.

Mystic was a beautiful bay gelding, registered name Into the Mystic, and as soon as I stepped into the barn, I could feel him reaching out to me, desperate to tell his story, wanting more than anything for Kelly to understand him. The process is different each time, the communication different with each animal I work with, but in Mystic's case, I could immediately tell that it was going to be an easy and fruitful connection. Mystic was as frustrated as Kelly, and he was eager to tell me everything that he had been thinking and feeling.

I stroked his neck, and he returned my touch with soft kisses. Almost instantly, his deep, soothing voice flowed into me. He quickly shared his history prior to Kelly buying him, told me his specific likes, his dislikes, and—perhaps most importantly—how he learns best. He also told me how Kelly could better communicate with him during their training. It was an amazing and gratifying experience, and I immediately knew I was going to be able to help both Kelly and Mystic.

At thirteen years of age, a high-end horse like Mystic is in his prime for mastering Kelly's chosen discipline: dressage. Neither of them could be called a youngster; Kelly was in her early fifties and had only been riding dressage since forty-four. That length of time riding is nothing in dressage—it is a highly demanding discipline that you could study and practice for a lifetime and still have more to learn.

Dressage is the art of movement and communication between the horse and rider. Consider it the *ballet* of horse riding. The object of the training of a dressage horse is to develop a harmonious and fluid-moving horse that responds in highly specific ways to almost imperceptible signals from the rider. The horse's physique and mind develop, as does its ability to perform, so that over time, the horse becomes confident, attentive, keen, and supple.

The discipline is exact, with no room for error. A horse must have three free, elastic, and regular gaits: a four-beat walk with no moment of suspension; a two-beat trot with a moment of suspension between each diagonal beat; and a three-beat canter with a moment of suspension following the three beats. It is the development of a happy horse and these three gaits that is of paramount importance in all the training.

Additionally, the rider must learn to sit in the saddle in a unique balance and use their weight, legs, hands, and energy to help their horse achieve these ends. Not just learning, but perfecting all of this is a long process for both the horse and rider, and during this time, a very special bond of trust and understanding develops between the two.

In our conversation, Mystic told me that he needed a rather laid-back approach to training. He even gave me specifics to tell Kelly on how to ride and train him, as well as specific mindsets Kelly could adopt in her work with him. Mystic also provided me with the exact things Kelly needed to visualize when riding him.

I could immediately see where the problems lay. Kelly was a type A personality, a very successful businesswoman, used to getting what she wanted when she wanted by way of her powerful intellect and force of will. She thought that hard work, discipline, and more hard work were the key to success in dressage. And Mystic? He was a type B—or even a C, if there's such a thing! But the bigger lesson here for Kelly was understanding Mystic's core needs and learning to let go, because relaxing on Mystic would be key to the pair's dressage success. They had to bond emotionally to perform, because when competing in dressage, horse and rider must be in perfect synch, with a well-honed harmony and mindset required for ultimate results. If the horse and rider operate in totally different ways, as was clearly the case with Kelly and Mystic, it doesn't matter how hard they work, how much they want it; they are never going to achieve the harmony required for a successful dressage team.

"So what happened? Did Mystic—you know—talk to you?" Kelly's face wore a mask of uncertainty.

"Yes. Very much so. He spoke to me as soon as I stepped into the barn."

"And what he told you," Kelly demanded, "was it useful?"

I smiled. "Very."

Kelly pulled her barstool close to mine. "Okay. Tell me everything."

As I told Kelly what Mystic had communicated to me, I could see that she was clearly somewhat skeptical—and why shouldn't she be? We live in a world of science, of data, of numbers. If you can't prove it or verify it, you don't believe it. And that was certainly Kelly's world, what she had used to become a successful businesswoman. But on the other hand, she had nothing to lose. As her husband had pointed out, doing the same thing over and over again wasn't producing the results she wanted. And worse still, it meant that her time with Mystic—time that was supposed to be fun, enjoyable, and a way to relax—was becoming the opposite: stressful and unenjoyable.

I'm the first to admit that not everyone understands or can relate to what I do, but my experiences have been so profound, the truth in them so self-evident, that I have learned to simply accept the communication I receive from animals. My clients have also learned to accept and trust what I tell them.

And so, as I sat and told Kelly what Mystic had told me and how I thought that would translate into her dressage work with him, she sat and listened, vowing to take it all on board and start to do things differently. When I told Kelly about Mystic and what he needed, Kelly laughed. "You just described my husband to a T," she told me. "I'm a classic type A personality, and Mike is an easygoing, laid-back guy—which, as you can imagine, has the potential to create some very interesting dynamics in our relationship."

Mike said nothing, just sipped his coffee and read his newspaper, but I could tell he was listening, taking it all in.

Kelly smiled. "I'll give it a try."

As I flew home from Atlanta, I had my fingers crossed that Kelly would indeed find a way to work with Mystic that encompassed all that Mystic had shared with me, and that it would renew Kelly's joy and delight in their time together.

It didn't take long. Barely a week later, I got a phone call from an excited Kelly. "It's amazing," she told me. "I have to admit, the first few days were hard. I had to really concentrate and try to remember what you'd told me—and I felt like I was being judged by Mystic, if that makes sense."

"Completely," I told Kelly. "When we first receive wisdom from the animals, it can feel like quite a role reversal."

"Exactly. But the last few days have become easier and easier," Kelly told me, "and today, as we went through our routine, I tried to remember everything you'd told me, and suddenly it was like night and day. We were in total synch. Everything just began flowing—there was no thinking, just relaxing and letting it happen between us. It was 100 percent better! I can't thank you enough," Kelly gushed. "I'm back to looking forward to my time with Mystic, and I have a feeling that our next dressage test is going to be very different from the last one."

Over the following weeks, Kelly checked in with me on a regular basis, keen to share her progress. She told me that working with the specific instructions I had relayed to her from Mystic meant that Mystic was more relaxed and confident, and that their relationship had dramatically improved. Now that Kelly was doing what Mystic was most comfortable with, they were both much happier and were finally working together to their highest potential.

Interestingly, Kelly also told me that in becoming more laid-back with Mystic, she had also become a bit more laid-back in her approach to her business, which—to her amazement—had also improved and flourished. The last time we spoke about Mystic, her tears of joy and pride flowed like fine wine as she told me about their most recent and impressive dressage test score.

Over the moon, Kelly was able to realize that when she allowed Mystic to work in the way that was best for him, not only did it guide her toward the results she desired, it enlightened and guided her toward some valuable life lessons that she needed to learn. The result was a win for both her and Mystic.

## Lesson

Every relationship has give-and-take, and our relationships with animals are no exception. They are beings with their own spirits, their own thoughts, and their own personalities and missions—and we need to remember that as we interact with them daily. When an animal is encouraging us to do something different, we can bet it's for our own good and for theirs as well. That's where the give-and-take comes in: once we get out of the routine of our own way of doing things, open ourselves up to new possibilities, and become aware of any area we may have blinders on, we are able to grow and better ourselves for the future. In the process, we will find that our relationships with our animal friends have improved, and we all will feel more confident and assured of our paths and our places in the world. What's more, we will experience an unexpected and profound joy and elation from letting go—after all, we are not in control of anything but ourselves. There is joy in surrender.

When communicating with Mystic, his guidance for Kelly came to me loud and clear. At its essence, it was pretty simple: "Relax; don't be so uptight!" It wasn't what Kelly expected or wanted to hear, and it certainly wasn't the easiest thing for her to do, but within a short period of time, that message had transformed not just her relationship with Mystic, but other areas of her life as well. She saw the interconnectedness of everything and allowed one shift to transform every aspect of her life for the better.

What Mystic taught Kelly is actually one of the most important lessons that animals can teach us. In our busy modern lives, we are often unable to slow down, whereas our animal companions are the exact opposite. I have often thought how wrong the phrase "it's a dog's life" is. My dogs have no cares or worries, nothing to worry about beyond their next meal, treat, or walk, and they spend pretty much their entire day doing things they like—eating, sleeping, or playing. Rather than us aiming to teach our animals—as if we are all-knowing—we ought to be looking to them instead to see what they can teach us. They often see us as uptight, tense, and in a hurry, never being fully present with them. They want us to stop, look around, relax, connect, and, as Ram Dass would say, "Be here now." [3]

We could all learn a thing or two from their approach to life!

## Reflections

Reflect on a time when an animal companion guided you to do things differently than you otherwise might have done, resulting in a noteworthy transformation for you.

1. When has the care or training of an animal companion led you unexpectedly to your own breakthroughs?

2. Has your relationship or bond excelled in light of these discoveries?

3. Has this learning changed your approach in some significant way?

## Exercise: Reading Their Chakras

Just like us, our animal companions also have chakras. Their chakra system holds the key to many imbalances in them, whether of a physical, emotional, mental, or spiritual nature. By unlocking these imbalances, we not only enable them to live in greater comfort and joy, but we can also unravel their untold stories, sometimes even more effectively than through animal communication. The simple act of clearing and balancing their chakras, more often than not, delivers us valuable information about—and communication from—them. At the least, working with the chakras of animals is a huge benefit when it comes to improving their lives.

---

3. Ram Dass, *Be Here Now* (San Cristobal, NM: Lama Foundation, 1971).

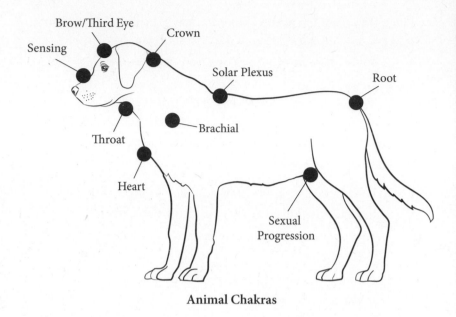

**Animal Chakras**

Depending on which school of thought you follow, animals have one or two more major chakras than humans: the sensing and brachial chakras.[4] I tend to work mainly with the seven chakras they have in common with us as well as the sensing chakra. I find it to be one that is often in need of balancing, simply because many of our animal companions are not only sponges for clearing our energy fields, but they often find themselves living in unnatural—or less than ideal—environments with us, which alone can create imbalances.

---

4. For more on the sensing chakra, see Diane Stein's *Natural Remedy Book for Dogs and Cats*, 6th printing (Freedom, CA: Potter/Ten Speed/Harmony/Rodale, 2012), 131. For more information on the brachial chakras, see Margrit Coates's *Hands-On Healing for Pets: The Animal Lover's Essential Guide to Using Healing Energy* (Random House, 2012).

For the purposes of this exercise, we will focus on the following eight major chakras: root, sexual progression (similar to our sacral chakra), solar plexus, heart, throat, sensing, third eye (or brow), and crown. Their chakras are very similar to ours in the organs and issues they relate to; however, some of the associated issues are understandably more geared to them as animals. The sensing chakra, which is unique to animals, governs the sensory intake and transmission of sensory information to the brain—in other words, how they filter experiences and deal with any and all sensory stimuli (seeing, hearing, smelling, touching, feeling, and even knowing). This is one of the reasons animals have much better senses than most humans. The color of the sensing chakra is silver-blue, with the colors of the rest of their chakras corresponding to ours. It's interesting to note that their chakras are not located in a straight line along the spine like ours are; that's because most of them are four-legged.

The following exercise can be done as a visualization or meditation—or, if you don't feel confident that you can do either of those options, simply go through the exercise and pretend or act as if you are doing it (you will still receive benefits from doing it this way). We balance and illuminate our own chakras before we work on the chakras of our animal friends—from this place of balance, we are best able to read and assist them.

1. Prepare a space as free from noise and distraction as possible where you can relax, undisturbed.

2. To begin, uncross your arms and legs, straighten your back, and bring yourself into a relaxed and comfortable position—either sitting or lying down.

3. Take a couple of deep, cleansing breaths, inhaling through your nose and exhaling through your mouth.

As you breathe in, visualize breathing in universal white light healing energy and exhaling any cares, worries, fears, or doubts you may have.

4. Ground yourself as we did in the exercise in chapter 3.

5. Now, visualize a beam of white light healing energy coming down from above and entering your crown chakra, slowly filling every cell of your being with wonderful healing energy.

6. See the light meeting each of your chakras. As it does, they illuminate and balance like colored light bulbs: your crown chakra illuminates violet; your third eye, indigo; your throat, sky blue; your heart, green; your solar plexus, yellow; your sacral, orange; and your root, red.

7. Now have—or picture—an animal friend in front of you. One by one, in visualization—or, if you don't feel you can do that, in your imagination—take a "look" at each of their chakras: their crown chakra, their third eye chakra, their sensing chakra, their throat chakra, their heart chakra, their solar plexus chakra, their sexual progression chakra, and their root chakra. Once you are "looking at" their chakras, see if you sense any of the following, and make a note of them: denseness, an imbalance or blockage, a feeling, a symbol, a color, a message, or anything else of that nature.

8. While continuing to picture an animal friend in front of you, visualize infusing them with the same white light healing energy that you filled your energy field with. See it coming down from above and entering their crown chakra, slowly permeating every cell of

their being, illuminating and balancing each of their chakras like light bulbs: their crown chakra illuminates violet; their third eye, indigo; their sensing, silver-blue; their throat, sky blue; their heart, green; their solar plexus, yellow; their sexual progression, orange; and their root, red.

9. Believe, trust, and intend that this healing light will release any imbalances, blockages, or other unbeneficial energy, and bring each of their chakras into perfect balance, spinning appropriately and creating an ideal state of homeostasis within.

10. Take a moment now to sense and commune with your animal friend and see if you receive any impressions or messages from them or sense anything they would like you to know. Make a note of it.

11. Feel gratitude for this process.

12. Feel your feet on the floor, take a couple of conscious breaths, and come back to present awareness.

I encourage you to revisit this exercise often to clear and bring balance to your animal friends.

# section four
# Animal Companion as Healer

# Chapter 10
# Healers in Fur

*Whoever said dogs can't speak was never interested*
*in learning another language.*

~MARK WINIK

During the course of my practice, I have encountered many occasions where animals have helped their owners—and themselves—with health-related issues in surprising and unusual ways. One of the most remarkable of them is the story of Jamie and Lola.

Can your dog detect cancer? It's a fascinating idea and one that has not only been related to me by one of my clients, but also supported by recent medical research.

"My beautiful Doberman, Lola, had always been very close to me," said Jamie, "so when she started sniffing intently at one of the moles I had recently developed, I really didn't think much about it."

A few weeks later, Jamie went to the dermatologist for one of her routine checkups—because of her profusion of moles, this is something she has to do on a regular basis. But what was different about this checkup was that during her examination, the doctor also zeroed in on—and later removed—the same mole Lola had been almost obsessively focused on.

As she left the doctor's office, Jamie began to wonder what was going on. Was it just a coincidence? Or did Lola know something that caused her to focus repeatedly on that particular mole? When the tests on that mole came back as cancerous, Jamie believed she had her answer. Somehow, some way, Lola was able to detect cancer in Jamie. But was this a one-off, or would Lola continue to detect any cancerous growths that Jamie might have?

Jamie had her answer when a few months later, Lola once again began exhibiting the same behavior, and Jamie's doctor once more said that the growth in question was cancerous. It seemed that somehow, Lola knew which moles were cancerous and which were not. Jamie had a lot of moles, but Lola ignored all the others, only bothering with the cancerous ones. "They all looked exactly the same to me," Jamie said, "but Lola somehow seemed to know the difference between the cancerous ones and the benign ones. I vowed to pay attention to her every time she began focusing on a particular area."

Trusting Lola's instincts, Jamie began to rely on Lola for early diagnosis of potential problem areas. If Lola started to show special interest in a mole, Jamie made an appointment with her doctor to get it checked. "I didn't tell the doctor how I knew to make those appointments and which moles I thought needed checking; she might have thought I was crazy," Jamie says, laughing. "I guess she just thought I was getting good at recognizing the signs. But it was never me who spotted the problem areas—it was always Lola who made the preliminary diagnosis. All I had to do was trust her judgment and book an appointment with my doctor."

It turns out that Lola's gift is neither imaginary nor confined to just Lola. Recent research has emerged that backs up the idea that dogs can detect cancer in humans. Of course, we've known for a long time that dogs have an extraordinary sense of smell. Their smell receptors are ten thousand times more magnified than a human's, I believe because they have a sensing chakra, and this makes them highly sensitive to subtle odors we can't perceive. But does this mean that they are actually able to detect cancer? That's what researchers from BioScentDX set out to discover.[5]

They gave the dogs—four beagles—blood samples that were either cancer-free or from people with cancer. Dogs being dogs, one of the pooches named Snuggles wasn't interested at all. But the other three dogs completed all the tests and were correctly able to identify lung cancer samples with almost 97 percent accuracy, a staggering degree of correctness.

Scientists are now hoping that this canine ability could lead to new cancer screening approaches that are easy, inexpensive, and highly accurate. One way might involve using dogs' extraordinary scent detection abilities as a way of detecting cancers, or alternatively, if scientists can figure out which specific biologic compounds the dogs detect, they could then design robust—and hopefully inexpensive—cancer screening tests based on those compounds.

Jamie continued to rely on Lola for her cancer diagnosis until the day her dog passed on, and Lola had a 100 percent record at detecting the cancerous moles. Jamie knows that she may always have a problem with her moles, but thanks to Lola, she

---

5. Heather Junqueira et al., "Accuracy of Canine Scent Detection of Lung Cancer in Blood Serum," *The FASEB Journal* 33, no. S1 (2019): 635.10–635.10, https://doi.org/10.1096/fasebj.2019.33.1_supplement.635.10.

was able to spot the cancerous ones in time and get them treated promptly.

Fascinating, right? But the story gets even more interesting, because even after Lola's death, she continued to help Jamie. After Lola crossed over, she was still able to identify Jamie's problem moles, but now she did it telepathically during communication sessions with me.

It's simple but magical. In our sessions, Jamie points to a new mole and has me ask Lola, in spirit, if it is cancerous. Lola always answers quickly and clearly, giving me a simple yes or no. I then share that information with Jamie.

Does it work? "It's amazing," gushes Jamie. "Based on Lola's answers to Lynn, I go to my dermatologist, and just as when she was alive on this physical plane, Lola recognizes my cancerous moles with 100 percent accuracy." Jamie can't help but smile as she says, "I'm sure my dermatologist wonders how I always seem to know which moles need treatment, but I'm not sure she's ready to hear that my dog is my own personal cancer screener, even from the afterlife!"

The long-term implications of this are potentially huge. Although there may be no total cure for cancer, we do know that early detection offers the best hope of survival. An early and accurate cancer screening test could therefore save thousands of lives, and dogs could be a major part of it. Thanks, Lola!

Animals aren't just able to share information about their human families, however. They can sometimes also be the best ones to tell us what is going on with their own health and even the health of other animals in the family. A number of years ago, I worked with a much-loved two-year-old longhaired whippet named Ocean who had recently stopped eating and was literally starving herself to death before the horrified eyes of her guardians, Wendy and Tracy.

Wendy and Tracy took Ocean to the veterinarian, of course, but after running a variety of tests that were inconclusive, the vet was unable to determine exactly what was going on with Ocean. He then referred them to the veterinary teaching hospital at the University of Guelph in Ontario, Canada.

With the greater range of diagnostic equipment available there, they ran a myriad of further tests on Ocean over several appointments. These tests initially proved inconclusive as well, leaving Wendy and Tracy—and the veterinarian—puzzled as to what was causing Ocean to refuse to eat.

Upset and in despair, Wendy and Tracy decided to call me. Wendy was very familiar with animal communication and trusted that through me, Ocean would be able to shed some light on what was ailing her.

Wendy and Tracy called me and explained the situation, and I consulted with Ocean the very next day. I had no idea what to expect—animals often share surprising insights in the communication work I do, but even I was amazed when the very first thing out of Ocean's mouth when I began the session was, "It's my duodenum."

She said it in such a meek and mild voice that I kept thinking I'd imagined it. But she repeated it a number of times, each time saying, "It's my duodenum," until finally I realized that we didn't need to talk about it for thirty minutes. She was sure that it was her duodenum, so who was I to argue?

To say that I was flabbergasted would be an understatement. Her information was so specific—and to be honest, when she said it, I wasn't even exactly sure what a duodenum was! I knew that it was part of the digestive system, but I had no concept of its actual function or specific location. For a dog to describe her problem with such exactness and conviction was a new experience for me. Prior to this, animals I had worked with would often point out a troubling area in their body or name the bodily system or major organ that was responsible for their problem, but not name the more obscure, specific part in this way. But being surprised is something I have come to expect in my work, so of course I passed the information on to Wendy.

Fortunately, Wendy was a nurse, so when I told her what Ocean had said, she immediately understood what I was talking about. She explained to me that the stomach empties out at the duodenum, so that could very well be Ocean's problem. Wendy felt that this information Ocean had shared through me could turn out to be a crucial first step toward Ocean's recovery.

The following week, Wendy and Tracy returned to the hospital, armed with this information. Wendy knew that an endoscopy would be able to confirm Ocean's thoughts on the matter, but the veterinarians wanted to hold off on the endoscopy, as it was a more invasive procedure. They felt strongly that they should try appetite stimulants first. Wendy and Tracy took Ocean home and tried the appetite stimulants, as suggested, but there was no change; Ocean didn't respond to them. The endoscopy was therefore set up for their next visit.

Imagine the veterinarian's surprise when the endoscopy revealed that it was indeed the duodenum that was Ocean's problem after all. Once they finally discovered what Wendy, Tracy, and I knew to be the case, they were able to put a treatment plan in place that was the beginning of Ocean's healing journey. Wendy has no doubt that the information I received from Ocean was lifesaving.

Up until then, they hadn't been able to get to the source of the problem, and receiving that communication from Ocean was like finding a needle in a haystack as far as I was concerned. However, Ocean clearly knew better, and she made her knowledge clear to me in no uncertain terms. And while I would never suggest that animal communication is a substitute for veterinary care, there are definitely times when it can be a helpful addition.

While the story of the way Ocean helped heal herself by communicating the root cause of her illness doesn't currently have scientific research to back it up like Lola's story, its validity was confirmed through an endoscopy. The end result was that Ocean had a rare (for dogs) form of bacteria present in her duodenum—a bacteria normally only found in humans. Her treatment was medication and a new diet consisting of kangaroo, of all things.

The stories of Lola and Ocean are just two examples of the wisdom and healing animals can impart to us. Animal communication can bridge the gap between the knowledge of humans and the wisdom of animals, allowing for more powerful results with better outcomes. With that at our disposal, why wouldn't we want to make use of it?

## Lesson

Animals have an immense capacity for comfort and understanding our situations and suffering—a whole lot more than we may know. When an animal companion seems drawn to you when you're sick or upset, it's because they can sense it and they want to make you feel better in any way they can. In fact, they know intrinsically what we need and when we need it—and just like in Ocean's story, in my experience, they often also know what *they* need most. We just have to give them the opportunity to share it with us and listen to what they have to say!

Our animal companions will always guide us toward healing, whether we're aware of it or not. Animals can provide us with physical, emotional, or mental healing as long as we are open. It's up to us to recognize the depth of their love for us as well as their commitment and devotion to us in order to receive that healing.

Sometimes it takes witnessing a powerful transformation for some of us to reach the point of receptivity and openness to the gifts from our animal companions. While it seemed improbable, Jamie was able to accept Lola's help in order to monitor the condition of her skin, and she was grateful that she did. It's important to pay attention to those seemingly tiny things your animal friend notices, for they may not be so tiny after all. After experiencing Ocean's accurate self-diagnosis, it was much easier for Wendy and Tracy to put their faith and trust in animal communication and an animal's ability to help heal themselves moving forward. Your animal companion is ready and waiting with gifts of healing that just might change the course of your entire life— and theirs.

## Reflections

Reflect on a time when you feel an animal companion helped you work through a physical ailment or condition.

1. Has an animal companion ever seemed particularly attuned to a bodily issue you were experiencing?
2. How did they demonstrate this awareness?
3. How did you respond—and what did you feel afterward?

# Exercise: Receiving Healing from the Animals

Opening to and accessing the healing from an animal companion requires a deepening of our sense of perception and an awareness that is a combination of paying attention, being receptive, and learning to truly listen. Another important element is getting yourself into a place of allowing the healing to flow toward you rather than pushing it away.

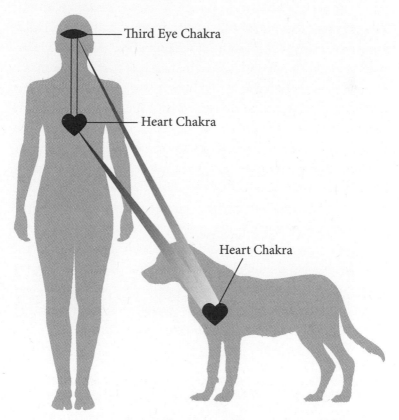

Third Eye Chakra

Heart Chakra

Heart Chakra

Over twenty-five years ago, at an advanced workshop at Penelope Smith's home in Marin County, California, my late golden retriever Jiggs (who was quite young at the time) gave me a specific technique to help us receive information and energy from the animals telepathically. This technique can also include receiving healing from them as well as sending information, energy, and healing *to* them. I call it Jiggs's Telepathic Pyramid and have been teaching it to my students ever since. I named it this as when Jiggs initially showed it to me, it was a purple pyramid with a white circle in it. I asked him how it related to animal communication, and he said that each of the three points on the pyramid represented a chakra that was involved: our heart chakra (right at our heart area, but along the midline of the body) and third eye chakra (at the brow) and the animal's heart chakra, located at the front of their chest. When I asked about the white circle in the center, he shared that it represented the "channel" that the information traveled through. The heart chakra is the center of unconditional love; the third eye chakra is the center of inner sight and intuition.

Again, in the following exercise, you will repeat some of the previous steps (grounding, quieting the mind, and opening the heart) to continue to build on your intuitive skills. To begin, take stock of any aspects of your life where you desire healing. They can be of a physical, emotional, mental, or spiritual nature. Make a mental note of them.

1. Prepare a space as free from noise and distraction as possible where you can relax, undisturbed.
2. Uncross your arms and legs, straighten your back, and bring yourself into a relaxed and comfortable position—either sitting or lying down.

3. Take a couple of deep, cleansing breaths, inhaling through your nose and exhaling through your mouth. As you breathe in, visualize breathing in universal white light healing energy and exhaling any cares, worries, fears, or doubts you may have.

4. Now, visualize a beam of white light coming down from above, toward the top of your head (the location of your crown chakra). Visualize it entering there and slowly coming down through your body, filling up every cell within you and illuminating each of your chakras.

5. Then visualize the light exiting from the soles of your feet and the base of your tailbone.

6. Visualize the light going down through the floor and any floors below you, connecting you and your energy deep within Mother Earth.

7. Now, bring your attention to your heart center (or heart chakra). Picture two small "French doors," roughly five to six inches in height, in the area of your heart chakra. These are doors that you can open at will.

8. Now, picture opening them outward in a way similar to opening the doors or windows in your home on a warm, sunny day. Experience the feeling of basking in the warm air and bright sunlight that come in, feeling great gratitude for this opening.

9. Consciously visualize and intend that your heart will be open to any information, in any form, that may come your way for the highest benefit of yourself, your animal companions, and all concerned.

10. Set a strong intention that simply by doing this exercise, your heart is now wide open and receptive to your animal companion's guidance.

11. Notice the way you feel in this moment—physically, emotionally, and mentally.

12. Now, I'd like you to visualize a tube or channel through which you send and receive information from the animals. Then, visualize a pyramid-shaped image that extends from your third eye and heart chakras to the animal's heart chakra.

13. I'd like you to visualize that the tube or channel is connecting your heart and brow chakras with the animal's heart chakra, forming a pyramid—this is what I refer to as Jiggs's Telepathic Pyramid. This channel is simply the vehicle through which the information, energy, and healing travel. Think of it like an invisible phone line, if you will.

14. Set a strong intention that simply by doing this exercise, your channel is open and clear to allow for free passage of the information you are sending and receiving. If you haven't used this channel in a while, there may be some cobwebs to dust off. If you haven't used it all, you may need stronger forces to clear it. Take a moment now to visualize clearing and opening it.

15. Relax into this new space and get familiar with it. See if any information or communication comes forth. Know that if nothing comes through right away, that's okay; this is a new space for you to explore.

16. Be assured that you can come back to this space often by simply visualizing this feeling and time.

17. Feel gratitude for this process.

18. Feel your feet on the floor, take a couple of conscious breaths, and come back to present awareness.

I encourage you to revisit this exercise often to receive healing from your animal friends.

## Chapter 11
# A Glimmer of Hope

*Until one has loved an animal,*
*a part of one's soul remains unawakened.*

~ANATOLE FRANCE

Despondent and hopeless, Megan sat cross-legged in the middle of her living room floor, utterly alone. Tears streamed down her face, blurring the label of the pill bottle she held with shaking hands. How had her life come to this point? Was this really the way she wanted it to end?

What she had intended to be a fresh start, a time and an opportunity to start over, had turned into an ongoing nightmare that she couldn't seem to escape. No matter what she did, her secret life of addictions and shame kept rearing its ugly head. Megan had never really considered herself suicidal, but it seemed there was no other way out. Her life had spiraled out of control, and Megan felt thoroughly powerless to stop it. She told herself that everyone would be better off without her, no one would miss her. She had no friends to speak of, and her family couldn't be bothered with her and her problems. Suicide was the best option, she thought, the simplest and easiest way to put herself—and everyone else—out of her misery.

She had been thinking about it for weeks, edging toward it, then backing off, but now, this was the day—Megan was going to go through with it, and nothing was going to stop her. It mattered not that she was just twenty-five years old. She had already lived a lifetime of experiences, many of which felt negative. Maybe her thoughts weren't rational, but Megan could only see the darkness and the steep slope her life had spiraled down as her depression increasingly consumed her.

But as Megan slumped down to the floor and covered her eyes with the arm that held the bottle of pills, she felt a little tug on the hem of her shirt. She ignored it at first, but the second time, the pull was stronger, and Megan opened her eyes to see a tiny feline face peering closely into hers. It was a moment that would change her life forever.

Megan had come to Miami Beach from DC thinking that she could leave her addictions and problems behind. Being the VIP manager of the largest nightclub in the city had certainly had its perks, but its accompanying lifestyle of alcohol and drugs wasn't one of them. Megan had gotten mixed in with the wrong crowd in her early twenties, but she figured that getting out of the city would give her a redo in a new home.

Sadly, however, the lifestyle will follow you anywhere if you gravitate toward it. It doesn't matter where you work, live, or spend your free time—what you seek, you will find. It's estimated that over eighty thousand people die from alcohol abuse in America each year, and almost as many from drugs, and having worked in a nightclub, Megan had seen some of that firsthand. It hadn't occured to her at the time that she might one day be among those numbers.

Miami Beach was probably not the best choice for her attempted do-over, however. Its sun, sand, and constant party atmosphere simply fueled her depression, though she couldn't see it at the time.

Megan got a job at a tattoo studio, which was going well—as long as she showed up for work on a regular basis. Megan wasn't on the verge of being fired yet, but no employer likes it when employees regularly call in or no-show. But as the days wore on, Megan felt less and less like doing anything at all, much less working.

Of course, she knew she had a problem. She had already seen psychiatrists, addiction specialists, counselors … you name it, but she just couldn't seem to break out of it. She had gone through five years of addiction off and on, and while some people suffer much longer, Megan had reached the end of the line. She should've been having the time of her life, she told herself, not suffering in misery.

To make matters worse, her new doctor in Miami Beach had given her a prescription for a medicine that she had taken every day of her life, but for some reason it was not agreeing with her this time. It felt like just another problem in her life at the worst time.

Megan had been born with a disorder called congenital adrenal hyperplasia, a rare condition where the adrenal glands are underactive and don't produce key enzymes and hormones. One of those hormones is cortisol, which regulates the stress in your body and the immune response to illness or injury. The medication needed to treat this condition is steroids, which come with their own list of potential side effects.

Thankfully, the regulation of Megan's condition was simple; as long as she took a consistent dose of 0.25 milligrams of cortisone daily, she felt fine.

However, if something causes a person's hormones to change, it can affect many systems throughout the body. When addictions are added into the mix, the results aren't good. And that's what happened to Megan. A mistake was made in her dosage. As a result, Megan was prescribed 2.5 milligrams per day instead of her usual 0.25 milligrams, a whopping ten times her normal dose. Megan didn't realize the mistake at the time; all she knew was that she felt horrible—constantly tired, her mind reeling nonstop, fear and paranoia gripping her. Quite simply, it was driving her mad.

Amazingly, Megan was able to hide all her problems and look presentable on the outside. She hadn't yet made too many friends in Miami Beach, but the few she had never had a clue that Megan was a depressed addict, nor did her friends and family back home. Even her new Miami doctor didn't realize Megan suffered from addiction. She dressed conservatively and displayed few of the typical signs. For a while, Megan even hid it from herself, unable to face the reality of just how low she had fallen. When it all came to the surface, anyone who knew her was shocked to learn the truth.

Amid all her darkness, depression, and substance issues, however, a small shaft of light emerged, courtesy of a neighbor's rottweiler. It wasn't the rottweiler herself that was her saving grace, however; it was what she carried. One morning, as Megan was standing outside her front door trying to decide whether she could face work that day, the rottweiler came trotting up to her, dropped something at her feet, then trotted off.

Megan bent over to look closer and saw two of the tiniest kittens she'd ever seen. Shocked, Megan looked around for any clues as to where they had come from. The rottweiler had already scampered off, as if she had done her good deed for the day.

Puzzled as to why the dog had dropped the kittens at her feet, Megan peered at the tiny creatures. They couldn't have been more than a day old. Their eyes were still closed, and they still had their umbilical cords attached. Her heart went out to them immediately. Had they been abandoned?

Megan carefully picked up the tiny creatures, took them inside, and laid them on a blanket in a warm spot. Their high-pitched mews sounded so sweet and pathetic that Megan knew she had to help them. She ran outside and did a search of the neighborhood for their mother, but she was nowhere to be found. As she returned to her apartment, Megan knew that she would have to become their caregiver. They needed her, and Megan couldn't abandon them. After another check to make sure they were alive and comfortable, Megan drove to the nearest pet shop, where she bought a bottle and some kitten formula.

Megan soon found out that feeding newborn kittens is a lot of work. Although they were demanding, the new visitors gave her a sense of purpose. Megan felt like the mother of a newborn baby, getting up to feed them in the middle of the night, making sure they were warm, checking on them every chance she got. Before long, they had stolen her heart.

The little boy kitten—Teeny Man, Megan called him—never seemed to grow. He was a furry little black thing that just wanted to be held and loved. The little gray tabby was a girl, and Megan just called her Kitty. She grew much faster. In the first few weeks, Megan could swear she'd grown a little bit every time she was away at work. But though Teeny Man stayed small, like a preemie, his character more than made up for it.

Although Megan couldn't provide everything their mother would have given them, she tried her hardest. She played with them, fed them, and cleaned them up after the bottle feedings got messy, which they inevitably did with two rambunctious kittens vying for her attention. Megan felt a sense of satisfaction knowing that she'd kept them alive and was giving them a home. Their adorable little faces told her they appreciated it, and though Megan didn't realize it at the time, she could see just how good the process was for her when she looked back.

But as the weeks went on, her problems didn't go away. Her mental health and addiction issues overshadowed any of the progress she had made. Despite the fact that she continued going to her therapist and addiction specialist, when you've lived a painful life, all you want to do is escape from it. Self-medicating through substances only serves to make the pain worse in the end, however, and eventually Megan couldn't eat, couldn't sleep, and couldn't function in any meaningful way.

As Megan lay on the kitchen floor on that fateful night, clutching the bottle of pills, she knew that she had hit rock bottom. Megan was ready to throw in the towel; she could see no other option. She was so blinded by the darkness in her life that she couldn't see any semblance of light.

It was at that moment when the kittens intervened, sending an unexpected shaft of light into the dark recesses of Megan's mind, biting and pawing at her clothes as Megan lay crying on the floor. One on each side, they pulled and tugged with all their might, meowing their hearts out. "Go away," Megan croaked through her tears, but they would not be dissuaded. In fact, they simply started pulling harder.

All Megan wanted was to be left alone to exit this world in peace, to find relief from the irrational thoughts that held her captive. She was tired of being addicted, tired of feeling crazy, and most of all, tired of being tired. Megan was utterly spent.

But as she lay on the floor, it occurred to her what Teeny Man and Kitty were doing. *They wanted her to live!* Megan had vowed to herself that she wouldn't abandon them, and wasn't that the very thing she was about to do? Who would take care of them if Megan took her own life? They needed her. The realization came over her like a wave, and for one bizarre but enlightening moment, it was like Megan was seeing her life from someone else's perspective. She did have purpose and meaning in her life; she just needed to see it. The kittens trusted and relied on her, and they were clearly trying to communicate to her that she should stick around.

Sitting up, Megan took a deep breath and chucked the pill bottle as far away as she could. The instant she did so, both the little kittens clambered up into her lap and fell asleep. Their message was clear: *Don't do what you're thinking of! We need you.* And as soon as they sensed that Megan wasn't going to go through with it, they went from meowing louder than Megan had ever heard to cuddling up, asleep in her lap. *It's almost as though they wore themselves out saving my life,* thought Megan.

That was the moment that allowed her to continue, to move forward to where she is today. Her intuition clicked in, and Megan made a plan for her life. Within a few months and after a lot of hard work, everything had changed. She had regained her health and worked diligently on her recovery toward an addiction-free lifestyle. It wasn't easy, but with a lot of help, Megan was able to get her life on track.

Megan firmly believes that sometimes, making up your mind to change your life can be the catalyst you need. That's not to say she doesn't believe in getting help, nor does she want to communicate to anyone that they should head to the pet rescue in lieu of therapy. Counselors, psychiatrists, and medication are all very beneficial and exist for a reason. But there's also a reason that animal therapy exists; sometimes pets can love and connect with us in unexpected ways.

Once Megan felt more on track, she moved to the jungle in Costa Rica for a year. *If you're going to change, why not make it a big one?* she told herself. A friend took care of the cats for her while she was gone, and she took that year to heal and get healthy. Megan learned meditation, herbalism, and other healing rituals ... all the things she never knew she needed but clearly did.

When Megan returned to the states, she moved to DC to be around family and friends, and her cats came with her. She is now a community herbalist, growing herbs and making medicine to give to her community free of charge. She also spends a lot of time working with animal rescues and fostering cats at her home.

Megan now has five cats in addition to the ones she fosters and takes in to be spayed or neutered. She's even had a few foster dogs over the years! The joy Megan receives from her work parallels the joy those two tiny kittens gave her so many years ago, and Megan wants to give back as much as she can.

Thinking back on her life with them, Megan believes it was divine intervention that caused the rottweiler to bring the kittens to her. She could've chosen anyone in the area to leave them with, but somehow she knew that Megan was the right one, the person who needed them as much as they needed her.

The connection Megan felt with Teeny Man and Kitty was solid; they were kindred spirits. Megan believes that animals have a special sense, especially with certain people. Anytime Megan was sick or not feeling well, Teeny Man and Kitty would come comfort her. If she had a fever, they'd wrap themselves around her head and groom her. When Megan was sad and depressed, they cheered her up. They just knew.

Kitty lived with her for twenty-one years, and Megan has her ashes on her mantel to this day. Teeny Man, who never did get very big, only lived to age five. While Kitty and Megan were devastated by his loss at the time, in retrospect, Megan can't help but think that he had fulfilled his purpose here on Earth in his short life. He was here for the time and reason he was needed, and that was more than enough.

## Lesson

Animals offer us healing energy and support during times of stress, pain, or illness. Their subtle nuances and comforting nudges are their ways of reminding us that there is more to life than our suffering, and we can overcome all with their help. The healing vibes of an animal can be therapeutic in many ways, showing us that they and the universe are looking out for us and that we will be healed from our hurts if we allow the help into our lives. Animals are there for a purpose, and this is just one of the many.

For Megan, the help of two tiny kittens enabled her to begin the process of turning her life around. Despite their small size and lack of physical strength, the kittens' tenacity affected Megan, proving that we should never underestimate the power of an animal companion. It's easy to feel superior as humans with such small animals and to take them for granted. But Megan got a peek at the wisdom and power animals have and can impart to us, and she allowed them to change her life for the better.

Sometimes in life, it seems that we go through a rough experience to come out in a better place on the other side. We are all works in progress, and we have to remember that there is no end to our lifetime of learning. Being needed by another teaches us a lot and helps us look at our lives in a different way. When we change our perspective, we will see that no matter how dark things may seem, there's always a glimmer of hope.

## Reflections

Reflect on a time when an animal companion was attuned to your mental or emotional pain and did their best to try to heal you.

1. Have you ever felt like the only one who really understood your sadness and despair was an animal friend?
2. How did that sense of understanding comfort you?
3. What did your animal companion do to demonstrate this awareness, and how did you respond?

## Exercise: Opening Your Channels

Sometimes when we are in a painful season of life, we may have a difficult time looking beyond ourselves and our problems—understandably so. Problems can seem overwhelming and can cause blockages in our energy fields that prevent us from communicating with animals (among other things). When we actively clear our energy, however, we will realize that we have been given many spiritual gifts to utilize; the "clairs" are one such example.

Our clairs are our channels for any kind of communication that is outside of our generally known senses, whether it be from the spirit realm, our guides and helpers, the animals, or loved ones on the other side. The four major clairs are clairsentience, which is clear feeling; clairaudience, which is clear hearing; clairvoyance, which is clear seeing; and claircognizance, which is clear knowing. They are gifts that each of us has access to; however, opening them commonly requires some attention.

A person with the gift of clairsentience may be someone who refers to themselves as an empath, as they often feel what others are feeling, both physically and emotionally. Those with clairaudience often hear things as if someone were talking to them inside their head—this voice may even sound like their own. Those with clairvoyance will see images in their mind's eye, as if playing out on a movie screen; in some cases, they may see clear scenes, and in others, symbols or color. Those with clair-cognizance just know things, but they can't explain how they know them; it's as if the knowledge of another were mysteriously imparted upon them. Your clairs are the senses you'll be calling upon when connecting with and learning the language of the animals.

Whether you realize it or not, you are like a radar tower, constantly receiving information through each of your clairs. You receive images, feelings, energy, and information like ingredients in a recipe. They come together to create an amazing end result that's much greater than the individual pieces of information.

Opening your clairs allows you to not only be aware of energy on a much deeper level, but it also allows you to have a better handle on your own energy: what you do with it, how you run it, the other energies you connect with, and the energies you disconnect from—the latter being just as important as the others. With your clairs activated, you gain access to infinite wisdom, heightened awareness, keen insight, deeper knowledge, profound perception, and true inner knowing.

We're going to do an exercise now to activate your four major clairs.

1. Prepare a space as free from noise and distraction as possible where you can relax, undisturbed.

2. Uncross your arms and legs, straighten your back, and bring yourself into a relaxed and comfortable position—either sitting or lying down.

3. Take a couple of deep, cleansing breaths, inhaling through your nose and exhaling through your mouth. As you breathe in, visualize breathing in universal white light healing energy and exhaling any cares, worries, fears, or doubts you may have.

4. Visualize grounding your energy field as you did in the previous exercises.

5. Visualize a beam of white light coming down from above and entering at your crown chakra. As it moves through your body, visualize it lighting up each of your seven chakras and exiting through your tailbone and the soles of your feet.

6. You are now connected above to Father Sky (the cosmos) and below to Mother Earth.

7. Visualize your heart center fully open and receptive to activating your clairs.

8. Now, I'd like you to tune in to your clairs one by one— clairsentience (intuitive or psychic feeling), clairaudience (intuitive or psychic hearing), clairvoyance (intuitive or psychic seeing), and claircognizance (intuitive or psychic knowing).

9. Do you often know things without knowing how you know?

10. Do you often sense things from others—either physically or emotionally?

11. Have you heard a voice within offering up useful information?

12. Have you seen things in your mind's eye that proved to be important?

13. When it comes to your clairs, which of them do you feel is currently your strongest: clairsentience, claircognizance, clairaudience, or clairvoyance? Take a moment now to place them in the order you feel they currently manifest for you, with the first one being your strongest. Make a note of their order.

14. Allow the knowledge of your clairs to settle into your consciousness.

15. Feel your feet on the floor, take a couple of conscious breaths, and come back to present awareness.

I encourage you to revisit this exercise often to review your clairs, your channels of communication.

# Chapter 12
# Daring to Be Vulnerable

*Only the truth of who you are, if realized, will set you free.*
~ECKHART TOLLE

One of my clients, Julia, lost her beloved husband Zeb when she was in her mid-forties. It was quite sudden, an enormous shock to her, and it left her heart in a million pieces. The last thing she wanted was to jump into another relationship, and as a consequence, she kept to herself for a number of years, unable and unwilling to deal with the thought of finding another relationship while her heart still felt so fragile.

However, as her fiftieth birthday approached, Julia decided that it was time to move on. Although she was extremely nervous about the whole thing, she let it be known among her close friends and colleagues that she was ready to begin dating again and even joined an online dating site. It had been over twenty years since she last dated, and she really didn't know what to expect, so she took all these steps with trepidation.

At first, Julia felt she was betraying her husband by even contemplating dating again, but her friends encouraged her, told her that Zeb would have wanted that for her, and that she deserved to be happy. So, she vowed to proceed with an open mind and to be open to what the universe offered her.

Over the next few months, friends began introducing her to potential partners. Work acquaintances asked her out for coffee. She even went on a few dates with people she met at the gym or through the dating site. And while Julia did have some fun, none of these encounters went anywhere. Every date seemed shallow and superficial; none of them encouraged her to follow up, and little by little, she became discouraged by the whole process.

Was it too soon? Had she finished grieving for her husband? Or maybe, she thought, was she past it? Was it that dating was best left to younger people? On some level, Julia still felt ambivalent about the whole process and knew she was probably projecting some of that when she went on a date, but it was so hard, such an unnatural thing to be doing after so long out of circulation.

Gripped by uncertainty, Julia decided to talk to her best friends about it. They were reassuring and told Julia that she was witty, cute, and charming; she just needed to be patient. But she felt certain that whenever she went on a date, none of these qualities seemed to come through. "What's wrong with me?" she asked herself again and again. "Why can't I find someone to share my life with?" Her friends were equally mystified.

It all came to a head on the night before Julia's fiftieth birthday. She went on a date that night with an engineer named Brad. He was a nice guy, very polite, but there was no spark, and Julia found herself just making polite conversation to get through the evening as quickly as possible.

At the end of the night, Julia hurried home and sat alone, staring at the TV, waiting for midnight to chime. Finally, her clock ticked past midnight. That was it. It was her fiftieth birthday, and she was alone. Was this how the rest of her life was going to be?

Despite the setbacks, Julia refused to give up, but after another string of false starts, she was getting discouraged. Looking for some fresh ideas and insight to help her move forward, she registered for a women's retreat that included Equine-Assisted Learning, even though she didn't really know what it entailed. "I'm not sure what drew me to it," admits Julia, "but I knew I needed a reboot of some sort, and this seemed like a safe space to get a clearer picture of what was happening in my life—maybe come away with a new perspective, my batteries recharged."

These types of workshops are designed to help people better understand themselves through spending time with horses, our ultimate mirrors. Participants take part in a series of simple exercises with the horses that, unbeknownst to them, mirror how their lives are currently working for them. Through these processes, their thoughts and belief systems may be challenged, and there are also plenty of opportunities to heighten self-awareness and develop and deepen critical life skills, such as truthfulness, openness, authenticity, trust, and communication.

In the first exercise, Julia found herself in a huge barn brushing Remy, a big sorrel gelding. All around her were other women, each of them at a different stall brushing a different horse. Julia was nervous and felt a little bit silly, already second-guessing herself, wondering why she had even signed up for the workshop in the first place. Uncertain how to behave around such a magnificent creature, Julia found herself reverting to baby talk and giggling self-consciously as she rubbed his shoulder and told him how handsome he was.

To her dismay, Remy, who was not tied up, responded by first looking away, then turning and walking away from her. Julia felt upset. She had come to the retreat hoping to escape from her problems, and now this was turning into a repeat of everything she had been experiencing in life.

To her relief, the activity soon ended, and the group headed outside for the next exercise. As she took in the warm sunshine and the soft breeze, Julia hoped that being outside would relax both her and Remy and allow them to begin working together more productively. He'd been happy to follow the other horses outside, so there was hope.

As the retreat leader explained the next exercise to them, Julia gave a sigh of relief. All they had to do was lead their horse over some poles on the ground, which looked pretty easy. The first couple of participants to try it sailed over the poles with ease. Then it was Julia's turn.

She took a deep breath. *I can do this,* she thought as she grasped Remy's lead rope. *In fact, anyone could probably do this,* she told herself. *It will be easy.* Julia stepped forward, feigning a confidence she didn't feel, and—nothing. Remy didn't join her; in fact, he wouldn't take a single step. "Come on," she said, "let's go for a nice walk." Remy barely acknowledged that she had even spoken to him, just gave her a disinterested look. Julia looked around. The field was full of other women who had happily led their horses over the poles, making it look as though it was the easiest thing in the world.

Julia glared back at Remy. *How come you won't do that?* she wondered. *Everyone else is doing it.* Julia took another deep breath, gave another tug on the reins. "Come on, Remy; let's go!" she pleaded. Remy looked away, standing stock-still, for all the world oblivious to her problem. *Maybe I need to be firmer,* thought Julia, tugging harder on his reins. Nothing. Not a step, just that impassive stare of a horse who doesn't want to budge for love or money.

*What to do?* Thinking fast, Julia rummaged in her pocket, finding half a granola bar left over from breakfast. She offered it to Remy, who happily gobbled it up. *Great,* thought Julia, *now we're getting somewhere.* Except they weren't.

When she stepped forward and tugged on the reins again, Remy remained stubbornly still, reinforcing his unyieldingness by turning and staring at her. *I will not do this,* his firm gaze seemed to say.

Nothing she did was making the slightest difference, yet all around her, the other participants had led their horses around, and they appeared to go happily. As she looked at Remy, it all became too much for her. She didn't care who was around, who might see or hear her; she couldn't keep her sadness and frustrations in. "What's wrong with me?" she wailed tearfully to no one in particular. "Why don't you like me?" She looked into Remy's dark, impassive eyes. "Why won't you even walk with me?" she demanded.

Her words surprised her; they paralleled her exact feelings about her dating woes. Saying what she truly felt, even though it was to a horse, felt strangely cathartic. Julia took a deep breath and leaned in closer to Remy. *Maybe there is something to this business of talking to a horse,* she thought.

"The thing is, Remy," Julia whispered, "I'm actually just plain scared. I know I'm a good person. I know I can be fun. But no one else seems to see it, and I just don't know what to do." She looked around, self-conscious, to make sure that no one was listening to or watching her have a heart-to-heart with a horse, but everyone else seemed busy with their own horses.

As Julia spoke, the dam broke, and she felt the tears begin to stream down her face. She couldn't stop them and just had to surrender to the moment, to the emotion. "I'm scared to be alone," she sobbed at Remy, cheeks wet, nose running. "I'm scared that no one will ever love me again. Scared that I'm just not good enough, or pretty enough, or smart enough anymore to have anyone love me ever again." She gulped back a lump in her throat. "I don't want to be alone for the rest of my life," she admitted, "but I don't know what I'm supposed to do."

Remy didn't move; he simply stared back at her, impassive, nonjudgmental. Absentmindedly, Julia reached up and stroked his neck. "I don't know what I'm doing wrong," she said softly, as if to herself. "I just want to love someone and for that someone to love me. Is that too much to ask?"

To her surprise, Remy turned his head toward her and nuzzled her arm. Just that simple gesture, that moment of attention, felt like the sun coming out from behind a dark bank of clouds. Julia laughed, wiping her damp cheeks on the sleeve of her sweater. "Is that all there is to it, Remy?" She laughed, suddenly feeling a wave of happiness that took her by surprise. "Am I just trying too hard?"

Remy stared directly into her eyes, then nuzzled her neck, her cheek. It felt wonderful. Caring. Attentive. Loving. Julia stroked his muzzle softly. "Shall we go for a walk?" she asked, turning and heading toward the poles. This time, Remy immediately fell in step and began walking calmly by her side. Once, twice, three times they navigated the poles, Remy stepping delicately over them while Julia walked beside him, chatting happily to him, expressing her hopes and fears, her goals and dreams, as though it were the most natural thing in the world to be talking to a horse. She was so engrossed in talking to Remy that she didn't notice when the activity ended, and they had to hurry to catch the other participants as they headed back to the barn. When it was time to leave Remy and move on to another activity, Julia felt genuinely sad, as though she were leaving a longtime friend.

Later, when she shared her experience with the group, she tried to laugh it off, but deep inside, she knew that something profound had happened. Without even realizing it, she had communicated her feelings authentically to Remy, and he had received them on a deep level. Julia felt that Remy had helped heal some deep-rooted wounds within her and understood that it was her willingness to be emotionally vulnerable and pour out her heart to Remy that had allowed them to make an honest and meaningful connection.

This is something I have been teaching in my workshops for a long time, helping my students make those deep, honest connections with animals, often with profound outcomes. Pretty much any horsewoman I've been acquainted with has known forever that horses are very in tune with us and can read our thoughts and emotions; that's one of the reasons I believe we are drawn so strongly to them. The same goes for any other animal when we allow ourselves to connect with them. They always seem to understand us; they're like personal "psychologists" on speed dial, but with the bonus that spending time with them leaves us so much better off than any therapy session I've heard of.

Interestingly, this is beginning to be backed up by hard science, with scientists in Japan recently demonstrating that horses can recognize human facial expressions and voice tones to detect different human emotions.[6] As I have found over and over again in my workshops, this can happen even when the person is not familiar to the horse.

Based on my experiences in my work, the research findings so far are very basic compared to what our hearts know and our souls confirm, and they will come as no surprise to anyone who has spent a lot of time around animals or attended one of my workshops. So far, proving what we "know" lags far behind what I see on a daily basis in my world, but it's progress, and I'm delighted to see advances in this area—limited though they may be.

So how did scientists prove that horses can recognize human facial expressions and voice tones to detect different human emotions? Their technique was simple—they showed the horses photos of happy human faces and angry human faces. When they viewed the angry faces, the horses' heart rates increased, they showed more stress-related behaviors, and they turned their heads to look more with their left eye, a behavior in horses that is associated with recognizing potentially dangerous stimuli.

According to Amy Smith, a doctoral student who co-led the research, this is the first time such responses have been measured. "What's really interesting about this research," said Amy, "is that it shows that horses have the ability to read emotions

---

6. Researchers in Japan have proved that horses can discriminate between emotional expressions in human faces. Similar studies conducted in Austria and Brazil have found the same ability in dogs and goats. See Kosuke Nakamura, Ayaka Takimoto-Inose, and Toshikazu Hasegawa, "Cross-Modal Perception of Human Emotion in Domestic Horses ( Equus Caballus )," *Scientific Reports* 8, no. 1 (June 21, 2018): 8660, https://doi.org/10.1038/s41598 -018-26892-6; Corsin A. Müller et al., "Dogs Can Discriminate Emotional Expressions of Human Faces," *Current Biology* 25, no. 5 (March 2, 2015): 601–5, https://doi.org/10.1016/j.cub.2014.12.055; and Christian Nawroth et al., "Goats Prefer Positive Human Emotional Facial Expressions," *Royal Society Open Science* 5, no. 8 (n.d.): 180491, https://doi.org/10.1098/rsos.180491.

across the species barrier. We have known for a long time that horses are a socially sophisticated species, but this is the first time we have seen that they can distinguish between positive and negative human facial expressions."[7]

As Julia discovered, as her openness, willingness, and emotions changed, Remy's response to her changed, allowing her to access feelings deep within herself. But did it make any difference to her life, or did it simply mean that she was able to chat with a horse and successfully lead him over some poles? After all, who gets dating advice from a horse?

Julia is the best person to answer that question. "Once Remy had helped me be emotionally honest with myself, I found I was much more able to be honest with other people, especially when dating." The result? Six months later, Julia was happily engaged to be married. "If it weren't for Remy," admits Julia, "I'm not sure I ever would have had the courage or the confidence to get 'back in the saddle.' I never would have dated or met my new fiancé Dave. I might not have ever found happiness. I'm so grateful for my experience with Remy!"

## Lesson

Emotional wounds can take a long time to heal, and sometimes it may feel like they never will. Unlike a physical scar, an emotional one can stay open and raw for years—decades, even—if we don't find the appropriate way to heal it. This is where animals step

---

7. University of Sussex, "Horses Can Read Human Emotions, Study Shows," Phys.org, last modified February 9, 2016, https://phys.org/news/2016-02 -horses-human-emotions.html; Amy Victoria Smith et al., "Functionally Relevant Responses to Human Facial Expressions of Emotion in the Domestic Horse (Equus Caballus)," *Biology Letters* 12, no. 2 (February 29, 2016): 20150907, https://doi.org/10.1098/rsbl.2015.0907.

in—they're our healers, guiding and teaching us the ways to get back to the core of who we are as human beings. When we stop, center, and ground ourselves, we open the door for the healing process, allowing our animal companions to share their innate restorative abilities. Before long, we find that we're healed, with our happy selves shining through again.

For Julia, like with many of us, she needed to discover her authenticity—to return to who she was deep down, her core being and her true self. This required her to let go of some old habits and beliefs—but more importantly, it required her to be vulnerable. For many of us, vulnerability does not come easily; we have all learned to put up walls to protect ourselves from future hurts and painful experiences. But we weren't designed to live confined within those walls, and our true selves won't flourish within them. Further, hiding behind those walls can prevent us from growing and being happy. With the help of an animal companion like Remy, we can learn to be vulnerable in order to bring our true selves back into the light where we belong, where we—and others—can see our worth.

## Reflections

Reflect on a time when you felt an animal companion "read" your emotional challenges or vulnerabilities.

1. Have you ever tried to fool an animal companion about your true feelings?
2. Have you ever seen any interesting parallels in your animal and human relationships?
3. How did the animal's behavior change when you became more honest and authentic?

## Exercise: Creating Inner Peace and Trust

We all need to reach a point where we recognize and become comfortable with our true selves, trust ourselves, and experience inner peace. Sometimes, to do this, we need to release blockages in our energy fields or clear away anything that's holding us back from reaching that point of peace. Diving a little deeper into energy is the key to achieving this.

Everything in the universe is made up of energy, including us. Any energy exercise we can do to enhance balance, integrate our brain hemispheres, and bring us into what I call a "healing state" is one that will help us connect on a deeper level with the animals. For this exercise, we're going to do a procedure called a Cook's Hookup. It's an exercise created by the late Wayne Cook, and it's one I learned while studying educational kinesiology in Toronto in the early 1990s. A Cook's Hookup is known to relax and calm the body, help with focus and grounding, and bring the energy field into perfect alignment, to name a few of the benefits it offers.

1. To begin, sit in a chair with your spine straight.
2. Cross one leg over the other at the ankle.
3. Place your arms straight out in front of you and cross one arm over the other so it matches with your leg position—both of them right over left or left over right.
4. Place the palms of your hands together, clasp your fingers together, and bring your hands down into the body and then up to rest gently on your upper chest.
5. Now, while maintaining the position above and with your eyes closed, we're going to focus on your breathing. As you inhale, consciously bring your tongue

to the roof of your mouth, and as you exhale, bring your tongue to the floor of your mouth. Do this for a couple of minutes.

6. For the next step, uncross your legs and place both feet flat on the floor, and unclasp your hands and bring your fingertips together to touch in front of you.

7. Follow the same breathing technique for a couple more minutes.

8. The length of time you do each of these steps is up to you and how you feel; I suggest at least one to three minutes in each position.

I encourage you to revisit this exercise often to bring yourself into the perfect state for communicating with and healing your animal companion.

section five
# Animal Companion
# as Catalyst

# Chapter 13
# Feeling Connected

*The best journeys answer questions*
*that in the beginning you didn't even think to ask.*
~JEFF JOHNSON

Bringing an animal into your family is a sacred commitment, not a passing fancy. But what should you do when you feel your life is leading you toward a path you feel is just not compatible with theirs? How deep is your commitment to the animal, and should you stick to it, even if it means putting your own life on hold or staying on a path that is detrimental to your health and well-being?

Such was the dilemma Cheryl faced. She had known for months—years, even—that her current lifestyle was grinding her down, that she needed to get away, make a clean break. But how could she do that and fulfill her obligation to Snow, her six-year-old white English setter/pointer cross? Cheryl had had Snow since she was a tiny puppy, eight weeks old and just an energetic ball of white fluff. They had grown up together, faced trials and tribulations, and had never been apart for more than a day or two. How could Cheryl leave her? But equally, how could she take her on the road with her? How would it work if she were on the road for an extended period of time? Was it possible—or indeed sensible—to take a dog on a road trip with no clear destination and no set end point?

Cheryl was already finding it hard enough to deal with all her other concerns. The extended road trip that Cheryl felt she needed flew in the face of being a responsible adult, of building a career, and, of course, of earning money. Almost everyone close to her had misgivings about the idea—a single woman setting off alone to travel the highways and byways of North America for months on end with no destination. It wasn't safe, it wasn't smart, and it was probably career suicide. Cheryl had heard it all and more over the past few months as she tried to summon up the courage to take the leap. But the more she put off making the decision, the worse she felt. Month after month, she was feeling more stressed, more unhealthy, more desperate to escape and discover her life's true purpose.

"I always knew I needed to take this trip," Cheryl recalls, "and eventually, this feeling pushed me to resign my position, rent out my house, and commit to taking off to experience the world." The final hurdle? What to do about her beloved companion, Snow. Cheryl wasn't sure how either of them would cope with an extended time apart. It seemed like a problem with no right answer, but in the end and after much heart- and soul-searching, Cheryl decided not to take Snow. It had been a hard decision, but Cheryl knew that if Snow were with her, she would demand a lot of attention—especially to keep her from her habit of snapping at people if she was nervous or felt threatened. How could it work?

Fortunately, Randy, a friend of Cheryl's who lived nearby, agreed to look after Snow for the six months that Cheryl was planning to be gone. It was a good arrangement, Cheryl told herself—Snow and Randy both liked each other, and Cheryl knew that she could trust Randy to look after Snow properly. But as the day of Cheryl's departure got closer and closer, Cheryl began having second thoughts.

"Snow and I had always been very close," says Cheryl. "I lived alone, so Snow was my companion, my security blanket, my best friend. She was always with me." When Cheryl sat on the sofa planning her trip, Snow was right there beside her, peering at her maps, sniffing her guidebook, trying to chew her pen.

When Cheryl went to the store to buy some supplies for the trip, Snow was with her, riding in her van beside her, sticking her nose into every new shopping bag that came home with them. And when Cheryl fussed and fiddled with her backpack and her new gear, Snow was right there in the middle of everything, sniffing, wagging her tail, and constantly looking at Cheryl with her firm, steady gaze.

Cheryl didn't want to read too much into Snow's interest and attention, but it definitely felt as though Snow knew what Cheryl was planning and was doing everything possible to influence her decision in Snow's favor. "It all came to a head the night before I was due to leave," Cheryl admits. "My bags were packed, my stuff in storage, everything ready to go. All I had to do was drive Snow over to Randy's place." Cheryl sat on the couch—one of the few furniture items she had left for the renter—eating pizza, her last supper before departure, with Snow watching her, as always. Then, Snow suddenly jumped up, trotted over to Cheryl, and shoved her way into Cheryl's lap.

"I was really surprised," admits Cheryl. "Although Snow was always very affectionate, she never usually sat in my lap. That was the point I became convinced that Snow knew what was about to happen and was expressing her opinion in the only way she could." As Cheryl sat stroking Snow's soft ears, she realized she couldn't do it; she couldn't leave Snow behind. She was taking the trip in order to relax, and that was what she had to do now—relax and trust her relationship with Snow, trust that sticking together was the right thing to do. For better or for worse, whatever extra demands it made on Cheryl, she needed and wanted Snow by her side. Snow had virtually demanded to come with her, and Cheryl simply could not ignore that. Snow was going on the road trip!

When Cheryl called Randy to tell him of her decision, he was disappointed, but as he later told Cheryl, not surprised. While he had been more than happy to look after Snow for a while, he admitted that he really couldn't imagine Cheryl leaving her behind. Randy had realized how difficult the decision was for Cheryl, how much she relied on Snow emotionally, and in his heart of hearts, he was delighted that Snow would be with Cheryl on her adventure.

Having made her decision, Cheryl spent the next few hours frantically repacking her stuff. Taking Snow meant a lot of extra work finding room in Cheryl's bags for Snow's food, her bowls, her bed, and of course her favorite toy: a stuffed rabbit with one limp ear. As Cheryl repacked, Snow supervised, following Cheryl around as though making sure that everything was being done to her satisfaction. When Cheryl finally collapsed on the bed, exhausted, Snow jumped up on the bed and promptly fell asleep at Cheryl's feet, her soft breathing eventually lulling a nervous Cheryl to sleep.

"It was almost as though she had seen what I was doing," recalls Cheryl, "and having seen her stuff getting packed away along with mine, she was satisfied that everything was going to be okay. Then she could relax and sleep."

And so Cheryl set out on her grand adventure with Snow by her side. Randy was there to see them off, with a big hug for Cheryl and a treat for Snow. As they pulled away from Cheryl's house for the last time, Snow sat upright on the front seat, alert, attentive, taking everything in, as though saying to Cheryl, "If I'm coming on this adventure with you, I'm going to be a part of everything."

It was a chilly March morning, the sidewalks and parks covered in a layer of thick, white frost as they headed out of town, and Cheryl felt a wave of relief wash over her as soon as they reached the highway. All the worries and concerns of the past few months melted away as the miles rolled by beneath her tires. She had made the right decision; now, all she had to do was relax and enjoy herself and allow the journey to unfold and work its magic. The original plan was for Cheryl to be on the road for six months, but as Cheryl says, "Heck, I had just barely begun to relax after six months." She was soon aware that she needed far longer to reap the full benefits of the trip, but with Snow riding shotgun beside her, she no longer had to worry about how long she was gone—she could set her own agenda with no one else to worry about. Six months, a year, more? It didn't matter.

Cheryl had initially worried that she might be lonely, traveling by herself for that long, but with Snow beside her, Cheryl not only felt safe, she never felt lonely. As any dog lover knows, when you have a dog with you, it's impossible to feel alone, and Snow kept Cheryl company as she traveled the roadways of America. "She also made me brave," recalls Cheryl, who credits Snow with leading her to meet a lot of people who ultimately became important parts of her life. "Snow was responsible for my opening up more and more to others," admits Cheryl, "something that I doubt I would have had the courage to do by myself."

Usually quite shy, Cheryl found that Snow was a natural conversation starter, an icebreaker at the parks and campgrounds that became her new home. Before she started the trip, Cheryl had a lot of anxiety about camping out in remote places. Snow banished all those concerns.

Every time they pulled into a new campground, Snow would immediately go off exploring. She would check out the site, introduce herself to anyone who seemed safe, growl at anyone she didn't like the look of, then return to Cheryl, her reconnaissance completed.

Cheryl quickly learned to trust Snow's judgment. If Snow clearly approved of someone, Cheryl was relaxed and comfortable around them. If someone got Snow's hackles up, Cheryl was wary and avoided them. With her four-legged, furry white radar at her side, Cheryl made a series of new acquaintances and friends, and she never ran into any trouble.

And even when there was no one else around, Snow made it impossible for Cheryl to be lonely on their travels around the United States and Canada. At night, whether she was snuggled up in her tent or lying out in her sleeping bag with nothing but a blanket of stars above her, Cheryl could feel Snow snuggled up beside her, her soft breathing comforting Cheryl as she drifted off to sleep.

With such an extended time together, Cheryl and Snow formed an even greater and closer bond, both of them becoming braver, more trusting, and more willing to try new things and experiences. With Snow trotting along beside her, Cheryl ventured into the high mountains, hiked steep, rugged trails, and opened herself up to the beauty and the wilderness they found all around them. She saw rivers and lakes, mountains and forests, parks and deserts, and she always had someone to share the joy and the experiences with. What started out as a six-month jaunt in Cheryl's van eventually became a two-and-a-half-year backpacking odyssey, most of which was spent living in a tent.

Cheryl had come from a high-paced job, and at first she found it hard to relax, but Snow was the perfect example for her. Wherever they were, whatever they were doing, Snow seemed to take it in the same unhurried way. And gradually, as time went by, Cheryl found that she was becoming more like Snow. Unhurried, thoughtful, ready to take and accept whatever each day, each place, each encounter offered, their moods and feelings seeming to fall into synch together naturally.

Cheryl was amazed at how quickly Snow adapted to her new environment, exchanging the comfort of Cheryl's sofa for the warmth of her sleeping bag, accepting their blue and yellow tent as her new home, and, ultimately, helping transform Cheryl's life back to a connection with the land, where she had spent her childhood. Cheryl quickly discovered how much she had missed the solitude, deep silence, and wide-open spaces.

Snow became a major part of the process—not just her constant companion, but her spiritual guide, her unruffled zest for life helping Cheryl recenter herself after years of stress and unhappiness.

The two of them never moved back to the city. When Cheryl's wanderings finally ended, they settled down in a small farmhouse in British Columbia, where Snow barked at birds and chased rats, paddled in the local creek, and returned each night to curl up at Cheryl's feet in front of the fire. Cheryl did her best to follow Snow's example, taking the spiritual lessons from their road trip back into her everyday life, never allowing stress to define her life again.

Following the interests of her heart, Cheryl used the photography she so enjoyed as a hobby and had developed over the years on her trip to build a wholesale greeting card and postcard business. Eventually, she returned to nonprofit management and worked as a licensed personal financial analyst as well as a clinical hypnotherapist. After adopting Snow's mentality, Cheryl felt more able to pursue what she loved and enjoyed, taking it one day at a time and enjoying life, no matter what she put her efforts into.

Even though Snow has since crossed over, Cheryl says that she is definitely still with her today in spirit, and she always feels her presence around her, particularly at significant moments or when an important decision needs to be made.

"I wanted to get away and discover what was most important to me, but I thought that meant abandoning everything," says Cheryl. "What Snow made me see was that she was one of the things that was most important to me, and that I could do what I wanted and still keep her in my life. That was one of the most enlightening things to come out of my trip, and I thank Snow for teaching me that lesson."

## Lesson

Sometimes we just need a little—or a lot of—encouragement to follow our heart's desire or our destiny. Although an animal may not be the first being to pop into our mind when it comes to bouncing an idea off a friend, given the opportunity, our animal companions can be excellent listeners and wonderful catalysts for change in our lives. When we truly listen to what they have to share with us and heed their advice, they can bestow us with encouragement and empowerment to enlighten and guide us toward the direction best suited for us. When we act on their guidance, we can move more gracefully onto our highest and best path. When we observe the way animals live, what's important to them, and what we may need to do to set our journey right, we are preparing to fulfill our destiny and our calling.

For Cheryl, it was imperative for her to go with the flow and trust the wisdom of Snow in order to get where she needed to be. This included trusting her own instincts as well as the instincts of Snow and, in many ways, letting Snow take the lead and accepting her guidance as Cheryl's copilot. As it turned out, the entire trajectory of Cheryl's life was changed by her seemingly small decision to take Snow along on her travels, which led to further fulfillment, a deeper sense of purpose, and greater happiness. We must remember that our animal companions are here to teach us to trust them and ourselves, and in doing so, we will be on the path to experiencing our greatest journeys and living joyful, fulfilled lives.

## Reflections

Reflect on an animal companion that you feel encouraged and/or empowered you to follow your passion or calling.

1. When have you felt encouraged by an animal companion to follow a life dream?
2. How did he or she empower you?
3. What did this encouragement look or feel like, and how did you respond?

## Exercise: Sending and Receiving Messages

As Cheryl moved through her spiritual journey with Snow, she learned to communicate with her on a whole new level. I am a believer that anyone can learn to communicate with animals— or at least connect with and understand them on a much deeper level. It's a skill that deep within your soul you're already familiar with and ready for—your only role here is to find your way back to that place.

The more you can approach this exercise with the enthusiasm and innocence of a child, the easier it will be for you. Think back to a time when you had an open heart and a vivid imagination and believed that magic was possible. It is in that place where your journey to communing with the animals will be accelerated.

In this exercise, we will be calling upon your trust, nonjudgment, and ability to let go and allow. The following exercise can be done as a visualization or meditation—or, if you don't feel confident that you can do either of those options, simply go through the exercise and pretend or act as if you are doing it (you will still receive benefits from doing it this way).

1. Prepare a space as free from noise and distraction as possible where you can relax, undisturbed.

2. Uncross your arms and legs, straighten your back, and bring yourself into a relaxed and comfortable position—either sitting or lying down.

3. Take a couple of deep, cleansing breaths, inhaling through your nose and exhaling through your mouth. As you breathe in, visualize breathing in universal white light healing energy and exhaling any cares, worries, fears, or doubts you may have.

4. Visualize a beam of white light coming down from above and entering at your crown chakra. As it moves through your body, visualize it lighting up each of your seven chakras and exiting through your tailbone and the soles of your feet.

5. You are now connected above to Father Sky and below to Mother Earth.

6. Visualize your heart center fully open and receptive to the information your animal companion has to share with you (as you did in the previous exercises).

7. Tune in to your trust level in terms of trusting yourself to connect with an animal. Imagine that it is represented on a dial, like the volume dial on an old-fashioned radio. Now, take a couple of deep breaths, relax, and go quietly within and ask yourself what "volume" your trust dial is currently set to. Is the volume barely audible, or is it booming loud? To have true heart connections with your animal companion and to send and receive information and messages to and from them clearly and with ease, your trust dial needs to be turned up high—and I mean HIGH! If you're currently working with less-than-robust trust, I would like you to visualize yourself reaching out with your arm and turning your trust dial up to a very significant volume. It should be one that speaks to the universe about how you feel about yourself—one that makes you feel audacious!

8. Now, clearly set your intention to communicate with the animals, both today and any other day you wish.

9. Call in your spirit animal and healing team to assist you with your communication.

10. Now, visualize Jiggs's Telepathic Pyramid (which I introduced in the exercise for chapter 10) extending from your third eye and heart chakras to your animal friend's heart chakra, forming a perfect pyramid for sending and receiving messages. Visualize a tunnel or tube connecting all three chakras. This tunnel is the

"channel" through which the information travels—
similar to an etheric phone line, if you will. Take a
moment now to intend that your channel is open and
clear to allow for clear passage of the information you
will be sending to and receiving from the animal. If
you haven't used the channel in a while, there may be
some cobwebs; if you haven't used it at all, you may
need an etheric jackhammer to clear it.

11. Call out your animal companion's name three times
    out loud or in your head.

12. Ask a simple question of your animal companion and
    visualize sending it through the channel.

13. Anticipate a fleeting response back through the chan-
    nel; very often, the response is so quick that you may
    discount receiving anything back at all and continue
    to look for an answer.

14. Your information may come in any form: words, col-
    ors, symbols, sounds, impressions, or knowings.

15. Try this process a couple more times with some more
    simple questions.

16. Express gratitude for any response you received and
    thank your animal friend for communicating with you.

I encourage you to revisit this exercise often to commune and
communicate with your animal companion.

# Chapter 14
# Nudged Toward Destiny

*I have studied many philosophers and many cats.*
*The wisdom of cats is infinitely superior.*
~HIPPOLYTE TAINE

Patricia had always thought that her ideal job would be playing with kittens all day long, but such opportunities don't exist in the real world. So, like most people, Patricia settled down and got a job, eventually becoming the manager of a large grocery store. She still carried that childhood dream in her mind, but the realistic part of her always wondered who could possibly think that such a dream could really come true. "Obviously, the universe did," says Patricia, "because that's exactly what happened!"

Patricia had always had a soft spot for animals, and they had always been a big part of her life. As a child, she had nursed a bird with a broken wing, tending it until it could fly again. Soon after, she convinced her parents to adopt a local stray cat, and from there, her childhood was filled with pets—everything from rats, to turtles, to goldfish, to rabbits.

Her love of animals—all animals—had continued into adulthood. She regularly looked after friends' animals when they were on vacation, and every night, she put food out for the local opossums. "I know a lot of people don't like them," says Patricia, "but I have a sweet spot for them, and life can be pretty tough for opossums living in town."

One evening, as she sat eating her dinner, Patricia heard the familiar sound of the food bowl being shoved around on her wooden porch. She jumped up right away—she loved to peek through the blinds to see her nightly visitors—but when she looked outside, she was surprised to see a stray tabby cat devouring the scraps she had left out for the opossums.

Patricia watched her for a moment. She had never seen the cat in the neighborhood before, and she knew most of the locals, stray or otherwise. From the way she ate and behaved, the cat was clearly starving. She was on high alert, keeping an eye out for any signs of danger as she scarfed the food down. As soon as the bowl was empty, she scampered off, disappearing into the darkness.

Patricia thought of the cat once or twice over the next few days, but she didn't see her anywhere around and didn't catch her at the food bowl again. Then, a couple of nights later, as she was parking her car outside her house after work, she heard a strange scraping and scratching sound. Patricia paused, but the sound had stopped.

Puzzled, she locked her car and began walking toward the house. There it was again! This time, it was more distinct—a frantic scrabbling sound, and then a faint meowing. Patricia paused, uncertain of what she had heard, straining her ears to catch the noise again. For a moment, all she could hear was the traffic on the freeway, a teenager revving his car down the block, and her neighbors a few houses down sitting on their front porch and listening to the radio. But then, as she turned back toward her house, she heard the sound again. It was coming from her next-door neighbor's garbage can.

Patricia approached cautiously, still not certain what to expect, tentatively reaching out her hand to open the garbage can. "As I lifted the lid," recalls Patricia, "the stray tabby cat shot out of the garbage can and landed on the front lawn." She paused for a moment, gave Patricia a cursory glance, and then trotted off down the alley on the far side of the neighbor's house. As Patricia watched her run away, she thought the cat looked pregnant, but it was dark and the cat was moving fast, so she couldn't be certain.

As Patricia unlocked her front door, she was deep in thought. Had her eyes played a trick on her, or was the cat pregnant? If so, it must be rough for a pregnant stray cat, thought Patricia, trying to find food, not having a safe place to birth and raise her kittens. Patricia being Patricia, her next thought was, *What can I do to help?* The answer was obvious. She put two bowls of food out that night—one for the opossums, one for the cat—then settled back to wait and see if the tabby returned.

It wasn't long before she heard the familiar sound of the bowl on the wooden porch. Patricia tiptoed to the window and was once more rewarded by a glimpse of the tabby on her porch, feeding from the food Patricia had left for her. As Patricia peered through her blinds, she was able to confirm her previous suspicion—the cat was definitely pregnant. She also looked less nervous than before as she emptied the food bowl. Had Patricia made a new friend?

She certainly had, and the stray tabby cat was a fast learner. The next day, when Patricia returned from work, the cat was waiting in her front yard. As Patricia climbed out of her car, the cat began meowing at her. "I took the hint," says Patricia, "and quickly put out some food for her." As Patricia watched the pregnant cat, she vowed to do everything she could to help her. Little did she know how much that would end up being!

The new routine went on for a couple of weeks. Each evening, the cat was waiting for Patricia when she got home from work, and each night, Patricia fed her. By now, she'd had plenty of time to look at the cat properly, and it was very clear that she was getting bigger by the day. It wouldn't be too long before she gave birth to her kittens.

Patricia wanted to do more, but she figured for that to happen, the cat would need to become more acclimated to her. One day, Patricia put the food down for the cat, but then instead of disappearing inside, she sat down on the rocking chair on the porch.

For a few minutes, there was a standoff. The cat was clearly not happy with Patricia's presence. She prowled the front lawn and eyed Patricia, and Patricia sat very still and studiously ignored the cat. Finally, the cat approached the porch, putting her paws on the front step. Patricia held her breath, but just as quickly, the cat stepped back, then sat and glared at her.

Patricia remained motionless, gazing off into the distance as though she didn't even know the cat was there. The cat watched for a minute longer, clearly hoping that Patricia would leave, but eventually, hunger won over. The cat trotted up onto the porch, gave Patricia another suspicious look, and then—never taking her eyes off Patricia—devoured the food she had put down. When she was done, she even took a moment to groom herself before trotting away into the darkness.

It was the breakthrough, and day by day, the stray tabby became more comfortable around Patricia, marching up onto the porch in a proprietary way to eat her dinner and staying longer afterward to groom herself and watch Patricia. Then one day, after she had finished eating, she walked straight past Patricia, and without so much as a glance, she continued right on into the house.

Patricia gave her a moment, then slowly climbed up out of her rocking chair and followed the cat into the house. "It took me a minute to find her," remembers Patricia. "I thought she might have followed the smell of food into the kitchen—but no, she was curled up comfortably on the couch, as though waiting for me to arrive so that we could watch TV together." Which was what they did.

As the two of them relaxed on the sofa, Patricia reached out a tentative hand, gently rubbing the top of the cat's head. Rather than being nervous or clawing at Patricia, the cat closed its eyes and began to purr. "I decided right then and there to call her Tabitha," says Patricia. "I'm not sure why; it just seemed right."

When it was bedtime, Patricia made a bed on the sofa for Tabitha from an old blanket, which she quickly curled up in. Patricia left her alone while she got ready for bed, but when she looked back into the living room, Tabitha was fast asleep. It seemed that Patricia had just acquired a new family member.

At that time, Patricia was training to become a Reiki master, specifically learning to work with animals. She was excited for this new opportunity to practice on this previously homeless pregnant kitty and her unborn babies.

Patricia would give her Reiki, especially on the belly, and was surprised to find that this formerly wild-seeming street cat was always so willing to have a stranger's hands on her belly. To this day, she will still come and lie flat on her back in front of Patricia, allowing her to touch her belly. "She gave me something to look forward to every day while I was at work," Patricia remembers, "and I asked her to please wait until my day off to have those kittens."

And what do you know—one Friday, Patricia's day off, Tabitha suddenly trotted into the kitchen, settled down in a corner of the room, and began giving birth. It was something that Patricia had never experienced before, and she found the whole process magical as, one by one, six tiny kittens emerged. Over the next few weeks, Patricia got to experience everything, from their first breath, to their first step, to the moment each one opened its eyes.

Within a few weeks, Patricia's house was filled with jumping, pouncing, tail-chasing furry life, all overseen by the infinitely patient Tabitha. Patricia found that sharing her life with her new cat family not only showed her that her purpose definitely was working with animals, but it also gave her hands-on experience each and every day.

Sharing your life with an animal—or in this case, a whole furry family of animals—is hard work and requires a degree of compromise, but Patricia took to it with gusto. It was a part of her life that she thought she had left behind when she grew up and left home, but now, she leaped back into it. The friends whose pets she had looked after over the years were more than happy to repay the favor when Patricia needed some help, and she soon settled into a new routine that encompassed not just Tabitha, but also her tiny babies.

"Everyone asked me when I was going to give the kittens away, but to be honest, it was not something that I ever gave serious thought to," admits Patricia. She was living her childhood dream of playing with kittens all day long, and the thought of separating Tabitha from her babies was too heartbreaking to contemplate. Tabitha had done everything she could to bring her kittens into the world alive; it was the least Patricia could do to keep the family together.

Over time, Tabitha and her kittens became not only her family, but also her greatest catalyst. Living with a litter of kittens is not always the easiest thing to do, but Patricia loved every minute of it. "They have been the greatest teachers," she gushes. "Words cannot adequately describe this whole experience." Soon after their arrival, Patricia made a massive life decision. She left her full-time job to begin her business of animal communication and Reiki.

Reiki, a practice developed in Japan in the 1920s by Mikao Usui, is a form of energy healing that works on the body, mind, and spirit of the recipient to support self-healing. Reiki treatments have been known to relieve stress, alleviate pain, induce relaxation, release emotional blockages, balance subtle bodies, and support other holistic and medical practices.

When performing a treatment, a Reiki practitioner transmits healing vibrations to the receiver. Some consider Reiki with animals to be more of a meditation that is done *with* them rather than a modality that is done *to* them. Reiki has been gaining new respect in the medical community, with some highly reputable medical facilities in the US offering patients Reiki treatments and analyzing the benefits of these programs.

Her new career path was brave, scary, and exciting, but somehow it felt to Patricia like the right thing to do at the right time. Having decided to keep Tabitha and the kittens, it felt like she had made the decision to dedicate her life to animals, and this was the next logical step. She never regretted it.

Tabitha arrived in August, two-thirds of the way into Patricia's six-month journey to becoming a Reiki master. She soon realized that Tabitha and the kittens were a built-in supply of eager Reiki recipients at home to practice on. While spending lots of time with and practicing diligently on her new feline charges, Patricia came to realize that they had begun teaching her how to communicate with them telepathically. It seemed that the more familiar she became with their energy fields, the more information she began to receive from them.

Animals, by their very nature, are more in tune with energy, both positive and negative—it's a big part of the way they interpret the world and evaluate their surroundings. A skilled practitioner with an open mind can thus learn to listen to them on other levels, becoming receptive to their spiritual wisdom and opening to their healing gifts.

Thinking of the days right after the kittens were born, Patricia recounts, "Those were the best days of my life," she says. "They were just so free. They ran on instinct and were so fearless." Patricia describes them as her "little energy barometers," educating her in patience and love and always letting her know whenever she needed grounding or energy work herself. They are her mirrors and teachers and have guided her toward the things she most needs to work on within herself.

After a number of enlightening conversations, one night, Patricia had a communication experience with Tabitha that she will never forget. They were sitting quietly together as they often did in the evenings (the kittens were asleep in a separate part of the house) and Tabitha began to show Patricia details of her life out on the streets. Patricia describes it like watching a short film in another language, but somehow, she understood it all. The images seemed to be flashing by, too fast to grasp each one, but each nonetheless leaving a clear impression and helping Patricia understand what Tabitha had experienced before they met.

The cats now play a huge role in Patricia's life journey and mission. She feels that she is here to help animals by helping their people understand and connect to the world of energy.

"Until Tabitha and then the kittens arrived, I wasn't able to piece together how my entire life's journey has led me to exactly where I am right now and what I am supposed to be doing," concludes Patricia. "It is super exciting to know and understand that I am finally ready to learn from these great teachers!"

## Lesson

We all have dreams, and we would all most likely give just about anything to follow them. But sometimes, life can get in the way. Following your dreams can be scary and nerve-wracking, and so many times, we put our dreams on the back burner or forget about them in the interest of being "practical." However, we may find that our dreams end up being fulfilled anyway—perhaps not in the way we expected. Animals can often be part of the divine plan that helps orchestrate and influence our lives. Sometimes it takes the nudge of an animal for us to realize that our dreams exist in our minds and hearts for a reason, and that we need to pursue our dreams in order to fulfill our destiny—and perhaps help others pursue theirs in the process.

Tabitha and her kittens changed Patricia's life exponentially. Patricia's experiences with the cats taught her to live in the moment, go with the flow, and appreciate each day as it unfolds. They ignited her belief in the magic of the universe, bringing together concepts she'd been wondering about for years into clear, understandable principles, resulting in a deeper perception of the way the universe works and nudging her toward her ultimate purpose and destiny. The more time she spent with the cats, the more she realized that her lifelong dreams and desires, which had originally felt like an unrealistic fantasy, were her true path in life. Tabitha's presence in Patricia's life was the catalyst she needed to begin her journey.

## Reflections

Reflect on a time when you feel you have followed the nudges of your animal companion toward your heart's deepest longing.

1. Has an animal companion ever inspired you to turn a dream into reality?
2. How did they nudge you?
3. How is the course of your life different as a result of taking action on these nudges?

## Exercise: Interpreting Their Messages

As catalysts, animals can affect our lives greatly—but when we learn not only to listen to them but to truly understand their communication, the transformations they inspire in us can be life-changing. Receiving messages from your animal companion is just one part of the equation; interpreting them is another. I shared in the exercise in chapter 13 that messages can come to us in a variety of ways: words, colors, symbols, sounds, smells, impressions, or knowings. Because of this, there are a variety of ways you can interpret them as well. As discussed in chapter 11, information can be received through the four clairs—clairvoyance, clairaudience, clairsentience, and claircognizance.

During your communication, pay close attention to the way your animal companion shows up for you and the way they present their message. When they show you something, try to interpret things from their perspective. If they are much smaller than you or happen to be lying on the ground, images that they perceive as huge may not appear so large to you, and vice versa.

If you hear a message from them, pay close attention to the details. It may be in your own inner voice or in a completely different-sounding voice. It can also be a sound that is not in words, such as a loud bang, thunder, a knock, or even music or poetry. The meanings of these sounds are unique to you and your animal companion; there is no "one size fits all."

Oftentimes, when my students feel that they didn't receive a meaningful message from their animal companion, it was simply the interpretation that needed further excavating. If you feel stumped in any way or that you aren't getting it, you can always ask your animal friend for further clarification so you can go deeper on the topic, or ask them to give you a message about another topic altogether.

Learning to communicate with your animal friends this way is a process, and I encourage you to stick with it until you experience success. Be sure to celebrate each tiny step in the right direction, and then build upon it with further communication sessions.

To help you learn to unearth the true meaning of messages you receive, here's an example of how one message came to me and how digging a little further and using the information in the exercise below helped me unearth what a dog was telling me (which, in this case, could have been very easy to misinterpret):

Decades ago, I worked with a woman named Joanie who wanted to further help her senior Bouvier des Flandres, Wyatt, who was on five different medications for numerous health issues. As I connected with him, Wyatt immediately showed me a red heart, and then he showed it coming toward me and breaking in two. It would have been very easy to interpret this message as a broken heart—his or someone else's—but my gut told me to inquire further.

Joanie was taken aback when I told her about the red heart, as she had just acquired a beautiful new heart sculpture in red glass to add to her art collection. I asked her if Wyatt spent time around it, and Joanie said, "No; he's like a bull in a china shop, and this sculpture is very valuable, so it's kept in a room he doesn't have access to." I felt absolutely no energy from Wyatt about that heart, so I knew I had to dig a little deeper. He did continue to show me the same image of the red heart, rather insistent that I interpret his message.

I told Wyatt that I needed more details, and he flashed me an image of a dog collar. I asked Joanie if Wyatt was wearing a collar, and she immediately said, "Oh my gosh, he is, and his collar has a tag on it that is red and heart-shaped; it's his rabies vaccination tag!" Wyatt nodded to let me know that we were on the right track. He told me that he no longer wanted to be vaccinated, as he felt this was the root cause of his health issues. I'm not a veterinarian, so I can't give medical advice, but I relayed what Wyatt confirmed and encouraged Joanie to consult with a holistic veterinarian about it.

Something interesting to note is that 99 percent of this communication was not transmitted through words, although many of the sessions I participate in are. All forms of communication are equally powerful, and it's important to be open to and appreciative of all of them to receive the full message.

We're going to do a Q&A with your animal companion to help you interpret the message you received from them in the exercise in chapter 13, so have some paper and a pen handy to record your answers.

1. Prepare a space as free from noise and distraction as possible where you can relax, undisturbed.

2. Set your intention to interpret the message from your animal companion with ease.

3. Trust yourself that you can do this and be willing to go with the first thing that comes into your mind. Unfold it and know that it is right.

4. Reconnect with your animal friend and revisit the communication you did with them in chapter 13.

5. How do they come to you? Do you see them, hear them, feel them, or do you just suddenly feel that they're with you or know what they want you to know?

6. If they're coming to you through clairvoyance, do you see them, or are you seeing through their eyes? Or are they showing you something completely different?

7. If you see them, what is their posture like? Do you see just a portion of their body or the whole thing? Are they highlighting one body part? Do you look happy and engaged or troubled and disconnected? Are they facing toward you or away? Or are they showing you something completely different? What are they doing in your vision of them?

8. If they are showing you what they see, what is it? If they showed you a color or symbol, what was it? What does it mean to you? Were there feelings attached to it? Colors, symbols, and impressions are unique to you and your animal companion alone—no one symbol means the same for all.

9. If you happened to simply feel that they were with you during your communication, was there a feeling or

emotion involved? This is something you would feel versus hear or see. Was there a physical-like tactile feeling of their fur? Did you feel their love? Did you feel that they were unhappy about something? Did you feel how they felt about a certain situation?

10. It can sometimes be tricky if the message you received from your animal companion comes in the form of a "knowing." This utilizes your claircognizance, where all of a sudden you know a fact or narrative but don't really know how you know it. It's akin to a divine download from your animal and is just as relevant as any other form of communication. How does this knowing come across?

11. If you hear them, are they speaking to you in your own inner voice or in a completely different-sounding voice? Is it bold and strong or meek and mild? Does it have an urgent tone or a more casual one? Or are you hearing something other than straight communication? Maybe it's laughing, music, or a baby crying.

12. Be sure to ask questions and stretch yourself to unearth the full message.

13. If necessary, revisit the exercise in chapter 13 to reconnect with your animal friend to go deeper with your message—there is always another level they can share.

14. Be sure to record your answers as you go or once you've completed the exercise.

# Chapter 15
# Achieving Dreams
# with Direction

*There is no greater gift you can give or receive
than to honor your calling. It's why you were born.
And how you become most truly alive.*

~OPRAH WINFREY

Can animals sense what we need and what's best for us? It's a question I am often asked in my practice, and the concept forms a key part of what I do and teach. Rather than simply share my opinion as I did earlier in this book, I think it's much more powerful to share the stories and experiences of my clients. A story can bring something into life in a way that simply giving an opinion never can. Shelby and Sugar Pie is one such story.

Shelby came to me a few years ago when she was at a crossroads in her life, and she experienced something so profound that it completely changed her life. At the time, Shelby had a successful career as an accountant. She had trained hard, worked hard, and was now in a position of great responsibility—highly trusted and well-rewarded. The problem was, she found it completely unfulfilling. Despite the success and the accolades, it was just a job, a way to earn a living with very little to get excited about. Like most people, she put up with it for a long time. Eventually, as the result of a series of events, Shelby realized she wanted—no, needed—much more from her work and life. Shelby watched as more and more friends suffered from stress-related ill-health due to work pressures and found her own work taking over her life, leaving no room for relationships or even relaxation. There had to be more, but how did one find it?

After much soul-searching, Shelby eventually realized that she wanted to feel passion for her livelihood, she wanted to use her gifts and talents, and most importantly, she wanted to do something that made her heart sing. "It was not just about my actual job," says Shelby, "but rather, my whole life. Where I lived, what I did for work, what I did in my free time, the relationships I had with friends and family. I wasn't happy, and I knew some-thing had to give."

Shelby was living in Birmingham, Alabama, where she had grown up. But with no living relatives in town, she had no real attachment to the place. "People think of Birmingham as an old-style southern steel town, but it is actually quite a pleasant place to live," continues Shelby. "But it wasn't where I wanted to live. I had always dreamed about living at the beach, waking up every day to the fresh sea air, sitting on my veranda watching the sun-set every night." A great dream, and one that many people share, but how can one make it come true? How would one live a life fulfilled in every way? The answer wasn't easy to find, but when it did come, it was from an unlikely source…

The deepest pleasure in Shelby's life came from the time she spent with her rabbit, a beautiful white ball of fluff named Sugar Pie. Sugar Pie had come to her almost by luck—a work friend had mentioned that her brother's rabbit had just had half a dozen kits, and she wondered whether Shelby knew of anyone who might want one. Without really meaning to, Shelby went to see them and immediately fell in love with one of them—Sugar Pie. She took her home with her that very day.

That was over five years before, and as their connection grew stronger and stronger, Shelby had become accustomed to confiding her deepest feelings and secrets in Sugar Pie. The rabbit had become her sounding board, the place she turned to when she was at her most stressed or unhappy. She figured others might think she was silly talking to her bunny this way, but Sugar Pie knew Shelby's heart and soul and was always eager to listen. Shelby found it comforting to share her most important dreams and even her concerns with Sugar Pie. Whenever she did so, she instantly felt so much better, and the answers she was looking for seemed to come to her within days.

This is a common feeling among my clients, particularly before they contact me. Many of them have spent years talking to their animal friends either directly or indirectly, sharing thoughts and feelings with them without truly understanding how deeply their communications are received by the animals or necessarily even believing in the process. They do it; it feels right, but they have a nagging doubt in their minds about whether what they are doing is real or something they just imagine to help them feel better.

So one day, on a whim, Shelby contacted me for a series of sessions. She had spent the past five years telling Sugar Pie her thoughts and feelings and realized that it was time to find out what Sugar Pie was thinking and most wanted her to know. Like many of my clients, she had some trepidation when she first contacted me, but at the same time, she felt so close to Sugar Pie that she was open to whatever information I could give her.

My connection varies from animal to animal, but as soon as I reached out to Sugar Pie, I received a torrent of information in return. Sugar Pie had many insights to share and was determined to take the opportunity to let Shelby know what she was thinking. She immediately told me that she was as concerned about Shelby as Shelby was herself, especially regarding how little joy she seemed to get from her career and how stressed it was making her. Sugar Pie was insistent that I encourage Shelby to follow her passion and find a career that really lit her up. When I told this to Shelby, a huge smile erupted on her face, and she breathed a deep sigh of relief for the pleasing confirmation. She said she needed some time on her own to ponder the magnitude of this message, which is a common reaction with my clients.

The following week, we had another session, and Sugar Pie honed right back in on the subject of Shelby's career. This time, she was even more persistent and very specific. She said that not only did she think Shelby needed a change of career, she even had a specific suggestion for what Shelby should do—she should open a gift boutique.

When I told this to Shelby, her response was immediate. "She actually said that?" she asked, gasping, eyes wide in amazement.

"She was insistent about it," I told her.

"That's amazing," said Shelby. "That has been a fantasy of mine for as long as I can remember, but I've never shared it with anyone …"

"Sugar Pie knew," I told her.

Shelby admitted that she had always been afraid to try it, afraid it was too frivolous an idea, that it might fail, or that people would think it was foolish. "How did Sugar Pie know this was my secret dream?" Shelby asked again and again.

As we continued, Shelby learned that what Sugar Pie wanted most was for Shelby to have a livelihood that fulfilled her, allowing her time to enjoy life and become the person she wanted to be. "Not the nose-to-the-grindstone kind of drudgery and responsibility I had grown up believing was necessary for success," Shelby relates, "but something that allowed me to actually have fun and express my creativity while working hard to achieve the kind of fulfillment I was yearning for."

Sugar Pie also mentioned Shelby's dream of living at the beach and strongly encouraged her to be brave, take the plunge, and really fulfill every part of her heart's desire.

Shelby gave it some thought and decided to take the leap—or hop—that Sugar Pie suggested. "It just felt right from the very first minute the information was relayed to me during the session," she said. "It was so strange that Sugar Pie had hit the nail on the head so completely; there was no way I could ignore it."

Of course, a move such as this takes a huge amount of planning—and courage—but at each crucial juncture, Shelby consulted with Sugar Pie. "My sessions with Sugar Pie had given me great confidence," Shelby says. "I had always felt that there was a real connection with her, but now I trusted it fully. I would talk everything through with her and trust that the answer I got, the feeling I got in my gut about what to do next, was coming from Sugar Pie."

After much searching, Shelby settled on Fairhope, Alabama, as their new home. A vibrant town of about fifteen thousand people that lies on Alabama's Gulf Coast, Fairhope has long been known for its lovely parks and its sweeping panoramic views of Mobile Bay. It boasts a real community feel, a myriad of quaint shops, and, crucially for Shelby, it has a beach. "I fell in love with Fairhope the first time Sugar Pie and I visited," recalls Shelby, "and the deal was clinched when I saw my first Fairhope sunset. I felt such a wave of peace wash over me that I knew this was the place I needed to live, no matter what it took to make it happen. I decided right there and then that this was the ideal spot for the two of us."

After a few months of planning, Shelby and Sugar Pie made the move down to Fairhope, all of Shelby's possessions packed up in the back of a truck, Sugar Pie riding along in her crate on the passenger seat. Despite the nerves in her tummy about making such a bold, radical move, Shelby was quietly confident that things would work out fine. As she pulled away from her old apartment, she immediately felt the stress that had consumed her life falling away, like a snake shedding its old skin. Rolling down I-65, a smile on her face as she sang along with the radio, Shelby traveled happily with Sugar Pie next to her.

Shelby had already picked out a location for the store, and a few weeks after moving to Fairhope, Shelby opened her boutique. And what did she name her new store? Sugar Pie's Gift Boutique, of course. "Even though I didn't dare tell anyone where the idea for it came from," she said with a smile, "I knew I had to give it a try, and since that moment, I have never looked back. I can't believe how much happier I am today than I was before Sugar Pie nudged me toward my dream."

Not only has she enjoyed every minute of it, but it has been very successful. Naturally, Shelby had been concerned about giving up the security of her safe accounting job. But to her delight, not only did the store work out, it positively flourished. "Within two years, I was making more money than I had working with my nose to the grindstone as an accountant," reveals Shelby. "Who would have imagined that?"

In fact, business was great almost from the first day. Fairhope attracts thousands of visitors each year, from golfers to snowbirds, and they began to find Shelby's store. Within a few months, Shelby knew she had a thriving business; she was becoming part of the local community. And the bonus? At the end of each day, she could sit on the balcony of their small apartment, Sugar Pie hopping around her feet while Shelby watched the sunset.

The boutique turned out to be a sweet deal for Sugar Pie, too. Not only does she have a shop in her name, but she also gets to spend every day in her fancy new hutch at the shop, keeping Shelby company and greeting the flow of visitors to Sugar Pie's Gift Boutique.

"It's become something of a ritual," reveals Shelby. "Whenever I feel like I need a little advice, I ask Sugar Pie." The process is always the same. After work, Shelby has her dinner, then she and Sugar Pie head for the balcony. Shelby sits and sips on an iced tea, Sugar Pie munches on a carrot, and Shelby tells Sugar Pie what she's thinking about. Interestingly, while at other times Sugar Pie will hop in and out of the apartment, when Shelby is pouring out her heart to her, Sugar Pie stays close and pays attention. "It's hard to describe exactly how she communicates with me," says Shelby. "I guess I would describe it as a process of me being open. I tell her what I'm thinking, then try to relax. I drink my drink; I watch the sunset; I smell the fresh, salty air; and after a while, the answer comes to me, and I know what to do."

For Shelby, the move has not just been about changing her job or changing where she lives; it has been a complete life overhaul. She has new friends, a new lifestyle—everything. "Sometimes, I look back and I can't believe that things have changed so much," admits Shelby. "I took the plunge and changed everything in my life based on the advice of Sugar Pie. It seems crazy even to me," Shelby says and laughs, "but I wouldn't have it any other way, and I know deep in my heart that I owe it all to Sugar Pie. I was confused, lost, uncertain—but Sugar Pie, she knew."

## Lesson

Change can be daunting for some and exciting for others. If we're in the former camp, we know deep down that we need to make a change, but we may not know exactly what it is—or we do know, but we're afraid to take the leap. What if our animal companions know what we need, how to go about it, and—most important of all—that we will be better off for it? What if their wisdom can help us find our passion, calling, and purpose—and we are oblivious to it or resisting it? The fact is, our animal companions know us as well as we know ourselves (and in some cases, even better!). If we allow them to, they can guide and direct us to the next steps that are best for us. Taking the time to listen and recognize these little nudges from our animal friends could mean the difference between happiness and frustration, fulfillment and emptiness. When we see these gifts that are given to us and embrace them, we will be more empowered to reach both our destiny and our dreams.

Shelby, just like many of us, was a little scared to step out toward her dream, and understandably so. It's daunting to venture into something new, not knowing whether you will succeed or possibly crash and burn—or somewhere in between. But our animal companions have insights that can not only help us take that leap of faith toward our passion, calling, and purpose, they just might lead to greater life fulfillment and happiness. And who would turn that down when given the opportunity?

# Reflections

Reflect on a time when the inspiration from an animal companion illuminated your courage and eased your path to change direction toward a dream.

1. Have you experienced a time when a dream that once felt out of reach suddenly became possible because of direction from an animal companion?
2. Once your animal companion inspired you, did you notice that the path to your dream became more effortless and synchronistic?
3. What actions were you inspired to take and what were the outcomes?

## Exercise: Opening to Their Inspiration

Our animal friends can put us in touch with and help us follow our life's wildest dreams and callings. Opening to and embodying the change an animal companion inspires and activates within us require a leap of faith and, often, an adjustment in the way we perceive life events and occurrences.

Sometimes, it's only in looking back that we can see how we were transformed as a result of being with an animal. So, for the purposes of this exercise, it may benefit you initially to think of an animal who is no longer with you on the earth plane—or one who has been with you for a large number of years—to get familiar with this concept. Whether you feel they helped you move in the direction of a passionate quest, nudged you toward your heart's deepest calling, or influenced your courage to make a much-wanted change, their wisdom can be invaluable.

The process of awakening to this concept requires deepening our ability to connect and communicate with the animals as well as a careful analysis of the life progress we've accomplished as a result of spending our time with our animal friends.

We're going to introduce a new concept in this exercise; we're going to ask for assistance from your higher self, the purest and highest expression of your soul, as well as your guides and helpers in the unseen realm, including the spirits of your loved ones on the other side (both human and animal). Each of us has a group of benevolent beings—a healing team—just waiting for us to ask for their help. They will assist you with your ability and intention to connect and communicate with your animal companion.

1. Prepare a space as free from noise and distraction as possible where you can relax, undisturbed.

2. Uncross your arms and legs, straighten your back, and bring yourself into a relaxed and comfortable position—either sitting or lying down.

3. Take a couple of deep, cleansing breaths, inhaling through your nose and exhaling through your mouth. As you breathe in, visualize breathing in universal white light healing energy and exhaling any cares, worries, fears, or doubts you may have.

4. Choose an animal companion you'd like to connect with.

5. Visualize a beam of white light coming down from above and entering at your crown chakra. As it moves through your body, visualize it lighting up each of your seven chakras and exiting through your tailbone and the soles of your feet.

6. Visualize your energy field being grounded as you did in the previous exercises.

7. You are now connected above to Father Sky and below to Mother Earth.

8. Visualize your heart center fully open and receptive to the information your animal companion has to share with you (as you did in the previous exercises).

9. Now, visualize Jiggs's Telepathic Pyramid: a pyramid extending from your third eye and heart chakras to the animal's heart chakra.

10. Call upon your higher self to assist you in connecting with your animal friend.

11. Call in any loved ones on the other side—either human or animal—to help you.

12. Ask for assistance from the angelic realm or any particular archangel that you have an affinity for.

13. Ask the animal friend to come forth now and show or tell you how they helped change and transform you during their time with you. This can be an animal that has crossed over or one that is currently on the earth plane.

14. Focus your attention on your heart and be relaxed, open, and receptive to any information that comes your way.

15. The information or image you receive may be fleeting, like a flash, so be sure to pay close attention and acknowledge information of any type (that quick first impression is what you're looking for).

16. Whatever information you receive, however tiny or insignificant it may seem, always have HUGE gratitude for it! Do your best to trust and believe in it.

17. You may hear words inside your head—in your own voice or in a completely unfamiliar voice—or you may see images or glean impressions or "knowings."

18. Allow any information you receive to flow through you and settle in, knowing that even if you don't know what it means now, its meaning will filter through in time.

19. Thank your animal for their time.

20. Feel your feet on the floor, take a couple of conscious breaths, and come back to present awareness.

I encourage you to revisit this exercise often to further open to the change our animal companions inspire in us.

# section six
# Animal Companion as Bridge

# Chapter 16
# Receiving Comfort from Beyond

*Everything comes to us that belongs to us*
*if we create the capacity to receive it.*
~RABINDRANATH TAGORE

Zoe, one of my longtime clients, had an elderly German shepherd dog named Sasha, whom she loved dearly. About two weeks after Sasha crossed over, Zoe contacted me. She told me about Sasha's passing, then revealed to me that she was devastated she had not yet received a sign from Sasha from the afterlife to let her know she was okay.

I told Zoe that I was sorry to hear what she was going through. I know how gut-wrenching it is to lose an animal companion as special as Sasha. While hearing from our deceased animals is a powerful way to relieve some of that pain, the absence of communication from them can simply make things worse. My advice to Zoe was to be patient, to not despair. Oftentimes, our grief blocks the signs our departed animals are trying to send us. These messages will come in time, I told Zoe.

What made this time particularly difficult for Zoe was that Sasha had always been very special to her, right from day one. Zoe had actually gone to the rescue to meet another dog, but the people at the rescue suggested that Zoe meet Sasha first. It was a beautiful June morning, and as Zoe got out of the car at the farm, the warm sunshine on her face, Sasha came hurtling across the yard toward her, skidding to a stop right in front of her, as though she knew Zoe was there to see her.

As Zoe knelt down, Sasha put her paw in Zoe's hand and showered her with kisses. As Zoe stared into Sasha's eyes, she knew that there was no need to see any other dogs. One long stare into Sasha's eyes and she was hooked! Thus began a beautiful, loving seven-year relationship.

Sasha was Zoe's comfort dog after losing her previous companion, Beamer, and she seemed to know it right from the start. At the time, Zoe was studying animal communication, and Sasha would just sit with her while she was doing her studies. The two of them were inseparable—whether Zoe was sad, happy, laughing, or crying, Sasha was right there beside her. When Zoe moved to another room, Sasha came right along with her. She slept in Zoe's room, and in the morning, Sasha would never go downstairs without Zoe, no matter how long Zoe slept in.

The two of them had no secrets, showed each other everything, and trusted each other completely. One of the dreams Zoe shared with Sasha was to move out to Arizona, and sure enough, Sasha was right beside her in October 2015 when Zoe set out to start the new life that she had always talked about.

Zoe even attributes Sasha with saving her in the midst of her crossing over. Zoe was on the brink of ruining her personal life when Sasha let her know that she was ready to go on October 12, 2018. Her timing was spot-on, allowing Zoe the time to sit back and think and make the right decision in her personal life. So, when Sasha didn't communicate with Zoe in the first few weeks after her passing, Zoe was both upset and worried.

About two weeks after our first conversation, Zoe called me again, happy, but with questions. "I finally received a visitation from Sasha in my dreamtime last night," she told me. "In my dream, the crematory delivered Sasha's ashes in a plain brown box. When I opened the box, Sasha was lying there, whole again, but she was empty on the inside, like a fur-lined pelt. In my dream, I picked her up and wrapped her around me like a big, warm blanket." Zoe wondered what this dream was showing her.

Through this dream, Sasha was letting Zoe know that even though she was no longer in her physical body, she was still with her, surrounding her like a big, warm hug from the spirit realm, always there to provide comfort when Zoe needed her. It was a beautiful metaphor and a wonderful connection, and even though Zoe was in a state of grief over losing Sasha, she was thrilled to learn that her beloved companion was fine and was still able to give her comfort and look out for her from beyond the physical plane.

Many of my clients tell me that knowing their animal companions are still with them in spirit and are okay is one of the most profound and powerful gifts they can experience; their animals continue to help them in numerous and important ways.

For me, this is one of the biggest messages for my clients—that the love we share with our animal companions does not end with their passing from the physical plane. I aim to help students and clients discover how our animal companions connect with us from the other side and let us know they're okay, enabling them to hear the heartwarming messages and experience the interesting afterlife anecdotes that I have encountered.

I also share how their animal companions often clear the path for them from the other side to help them with their success and goals and answer any related questions they may have.

I have seen time and again that our animals stay connected with us after their passing. People sometimes find it easier to feel them around soon after they pass, but they are equally able to visit and communicate with us long after they have crossed from the physical plane.

One important thing I discuss with clients is that we need to be open and aware of the signals we may receive from our animal companions in spirit, and we often must be somewhat healed of our grief from their passing to notice them. The animals show themselves in various ways, often through weather formations like clouds, wind, rainbows, and so on, or through a visitation in the form of winged creatures, including both birds and insects. In fact, as I sit here writing this, my beloved Carly, my late Maltese dog, just visited in the form of one of a pair of red-tailed hawks riding the currents right outside my office window, waiting for me to take notice. I was so engrossed in my work that at first I didn't notice her. She really wanted to get my attention and be mentioned here—I've never before seen hawks stick around in one place for so long.

When I communicate with animals that have passed, they always share with me that transitioning to the spirit realm is a wonderful feeling for them. They say that it is a feeling of being freed, of soaring like an eagle in complete expansiveness and joy. The number one thing they tell me and want their people to know is that they are okay. To them, death is not a negative thing, nor something they fear. It is just like the birth process, a very natural and inevitable part of the circle of life. However, people often fear death—both their own and that of their loved ones and animal companions. So, learning that their beloved animal friend is fine and happy and that their transition was a positive experience is both comforting and reassuring.

Since we are all so different, not everyone receives messages from spirits in the same fashion. I have found that there is a fine line between trusting that our animal companions' spirits are with us and delivering messages to us regularly versus feeling they are nowhere around us, and therefore not offering us any messages or signs. So, when people call me to tell me they have sensed nothing from an animal that's crossed over and are worried about it, I always reassure them and encourage them not to despair. Messages will come in time if they are open to them.

Another client, Penny, tells a tragic story with a memorable ending. Sammy was an exuberant and very loving little male yellow Lab, just eighteen months old when he was taken from Penny. Sammy had been with Penny since he was an eight-week-old puppy and had connected with her from the very first moment they met. Upon first meeting him, Penny asked him to give her a sign that he was supposed to be with her to help her learn animal communication. "To my surprise," recalls Penny, "he sat up pretty and pawed at my leg, which is normally hard for a puppy to do at that age. From that moment, I knew we were supposed to be together."

January 21, 2018 began as any other normal day, but it changed in the early afternoon when Sammy began jumping up and down at the door to go outside. "He had seen a red-tailed hawk fly across the ridge behind our house several times," says Penny, "and he was always desperate to go chase it. I opened the door to let him out, and he and my other four dogs charged outside into the backyard." That day, instead of running down the hill after the hawk like the other dogs, he launched off the ridge like he was jumping into a swimming pool. Penny thought it was kind of odd as she watched it, but she didn't think anything more of it until she saw the hawk make a half circle and swoop back around a little lower, like he was looking at something. She also thought that was odd behavior, but she didn't hear or see anything else to make her question anything further.

A while after letting all the dogs out to chase the hawk, she heard them barking and called them in. Sammy was the last dog to come to the door, and when Penny saw him, her heart fell—he was covered in blood, with more blood still dripping from his chest. "I scooped him up in a blanket and raced him to a veterinary emergency clinic without even knowing what had happened to him," recalls Penny.

The veterinarian immediately found a large hole in his chest. They took X-rays and did blood work and determined that Sammy had several broken ribs and a punctured and collapsed lung, along with major tissue damage. He went straight into surgery, with several blood transfusions, and although he now had just one lung remaining, they were hopeful that he would survive. However, after making it through the surgery, he passed away about ten minutes later, unable to breathe.

Later that day, Penny went outside to try to figure out what had happened. As she crested the ridge, she saw a large native plant with a broken branch about an inch and a half wide. When he had leaped over the ridge, he impaled himself on the plant, and the branch had gone into his chest just under his armpit, causing massive trauma to his tissue. He had then made his way back up the hill, where he hid behind the swimming pool heater to be alone to bleed out and die.

At the time, Penny was clueless to the fact that he had even been hurt, as there was no yelping, crying, or noise after he hurt himself. "In my grief, I just felt so blessed that he was able to come to me when I called him to come in, and that I was able to try to get him some help so he didn't have to die alone."

Penny was heartbroken at his loss because as a healer, she was hoping to help him with his recovery after surgery. After Sammy passed so suddenly, Penny asked her angels for help, but she received nothing. She felt that they had deserted her in her time of need. All she could do was pray, and though she tried desperately to connect with Sammy, she felt no signs—nothing at all.

Penny was in so much emotional pain and grief that she began questioning her faith, her trust, and her beliefs in all of her metaphysical work. "I have to admit," says Penny, "I wasn't sure I ever wanted to try to speak to spirits or animals ever again, or to even pursue my spiritual path any further. I even hated the hawks as they flew along the ridge, knowing they were partially the cause of Sammy's death." In short, she was ready to give up.

A few more weeks went by, and Penny's grief showed no signs of abating, so she decided to ask Sammy once again for a sign to prove that this type of communication is truly real. She was so down that she didn't think she would get a sign or message from him, but she chose to do a flame reading to see. A flame reading is an exercise that culminates in smoke and ash markings appearing on paper, which can often portray pictures. She soon found herself shocked and amazed that when she looked at the card, she could actually see Sammy's face in the ash. It brought tears to her eyes that he had responded in such a clear and dramatic way, assuring her that he was okay.

Her faith restored, a week later, Penny was thinking about Sammy as she was driving and was picturing him just as if he was in the back seat riding along with her—when lo and behold, a car pulled right in front of her with Sammy's name on the license plate. "That felt like a miracle!" recalls Penny. "Another confirmation of spirit connection being real."

With Sammy's death and the signs he has since sent her, Penny now considers the hawk one of her spirit animals, here to teach her, inspire her, and help her keep journeying along her spiritual path. Each time she sees one out in her yard or when she's driving, she says hello to her sweet Sammy and asks if he has a message for her. "It is truly amazing how many times the hawk has shown up for me when I needed help or clarity," says Penny, "a sure sign that my sweet Sammy is still there, still looking out for me."

So how do you know if you are receiving communication from an animal friend in spirit? The first step is in accepting and believing that it is possible. The next step is trusting that the guidance and teaching our animal companions offer us while they are on this plane can and do continue once they have crossed over to the afterlife. I believe that everyone can learn to receive this type of message or communication through at least one of a variety of methods. These include learning interspecies telepathic communication, looking for and noticing signs from spirits—including during meditation and dreamtime—or simply by osmosis. Lastly, consulting with an animal intuitive helps many people open their pathways to messages and communication from beings who are now in spirit form.

Many people have doubts or reservations about the messages and communications they receive, but I have found that some of the messages I've received contain information that I simply could not have already known, such as when animals who have crossed tell me exactly how they died or relay information about reuniting with loved ones on the other side, both human and animal—again, sharing things I would have no other way of knowing.

## Lesson

While our animal companions may no longer be with us physically, their spirits stay with us long after they have crossed over. In our grief, it may be difficult to remember this, but when we look for signs and communication from those who have crossed over, our hearts can be comforted. The bond of love and companionship is stronger even than death, and their spirits remain with us to help, teach, and guide us throughout our lives. We can take comfort in knowing that they are all right on the other side, that they're happy and free and looking out for us. The best part is that we can still feel and communicate with them, and they are the same beings we knew here on the earthly plane, our companions divinely chosen for us.

Both Zoe and Penny were looking for that communication, hoping to receive a confirmation that their animal companions were still with them, even though deep down, they both knew that to be the case. Not hearing from an animal companion who has crossed over doesn't mean they're not still with us or aren't all right; it just may require us to pay close attention and to wait for the right moment. When we are attuned to the possibility of noticing those little signs, symbols, and synchronicities, we place ourselves in the state of being receptive and open to them. They may not show up in the time we expect, but we have to have faith in the spiritual realm and trust the methods of communication from the afterlife. Despite the grief that comes along with losing a beloved animal companion, we can still be comforted from their spirit in many ways from the afterlife.

## Reflections

Reflect on an animal companion whom you were deeply connected to but who has now crossed over.

1. Were you desperate for a sign from the other side that they were okay?
2. What messages have you received from them?
3. Did this encounter bring you peace of mind and comfort?

## Exercise: Signs from Animals in Spirit

Messages from our animal companions in spirit are not only comforting, they also help us assimilate their transition from the physical plane to the spirit realm. They also prove to us that there is no death, and that the love we share and the deep connections we have with them live on beyond the ending of the physical body.

If an animal friend has crossed over and you are looking for a sign from them that they are okay and can still be present for you, an important step is to talk to them as you would if they were still here on this plane and ask them for a sign. You can do this out loud or in your head; they will hear you either way. Then, wait and watch with heightened awareness for a sign to present itself. This doesn't mean that they wouldn't send you a sign without asking, but I find that when we ask, we're more consciously involved in the process and therefore more apt to notice it when they do.

Here are some of the signs that I've received from animals on the other side. Some are more common than others, and this is just a partial list: playing with electricity by flickering the lights or television, sending shapes in clouds, catching a glimpse of them out of the corner of my eye, dreaming vividly about them, hearing an audible bark or whine in the night, seeing a foot-print impression in a fluffy duvet, receiving a feather or coin and knowing it was sent by them, noticing a bird—such as a red-tailed hawk or cardinal—and knowing it's them, or having them inhabit the body of another living animal companion for a short visit.

1. Using the information above, take a moment now to journal about any experiences you've had where you feel an animal companion has sent or showed you a sign.

2. Write down an experience you've had that could have been a sign, even if you're not sure. If it's coming into your consciousness, my feeling is that it is a sign.

3. Take a moment now to tune in to the spirit of an animal companion that is in the spiritual realm and ask them to bring you a sign.

4. Fully intend that they will, and be on the lookout for it.

My hope is that working with this will help awaken you to possibilities with your own beloved animal companions in spirit. If you're in the early stages after their transition and are bogged down in grief from their loss, it can block your ability to notice their signs, so be gentle with yourself and be sure to allow yourself plenty of time to heal before expecting to receive your message.

## Chapter 17
# Overcoming Despair

*Those who teach us the most*
*about humanity aren't always humans.*

~DONALD HICKS

In my practice, I have often observed that certain animals come into people's lives at specific times and for specific reasons. It may not always be obvious in the moment. In fact, it often seems that these happenings occur at the most inopportune times. But as we get to know these animal friends, our connections with them can turn into profound, even life-changing experiences, timed perfectly for what we needed in that moment. That was certainly Carys's situation.

It was about seven months into one of the most heartbreaking times of Carys's life when she discovered a little black kitten hiding under her storage trailer, meowing loudly. It was a tiny baby, nervous, skittish, its coat in need of a brush; normally, Carys would have taken it in to care for it immediately. But this wasn't a normal time for Carys.

"My heart was completely broken and aching with sadness and loss from the accumulation of grief," says Carys, "and I had sworn that I would not seek another animal friend for a while."

With her life and her mind dominated by her current situation, Carys's first thought was, *Please, kitty, go home. I just can't begin to help you right now.* She hurried back into her house, hoping that the kitten would be gone the next time she went outside.

Her father had just entered the final stages of a terminal illness; she had recently lost two beloved horses to old age; and her current cat, fourteen-year-old Finn, was weakening by the day. It felt like Carys's life was becoming increasingly difficult, and the last thing she needed was another mouth to feed, another fragile life to be responsible for.

Although she had been around animals all her life, Carys had never gotten used to them dying—and she struggled as much or more with the loss of people. She had grown up with dogs, cats, and horses too numerous to count, so you might have thought that the cycle of life and death would have become something she was accustomed to by now. Her father bred and raised thoroughbreds, so she had always been around a variety of horses—from broodmares to frisky colts, the whole works. But somehow, she had never managed to reconcile the heartbreak and inevitable ending that always came from sharing her life with them. And so, the recent loss of her two favorite horses, one after the other, had gutted her, and she had yet to get over their passing.

As if losing her beloved horses wasn't bad enough, Carys was also her father's primary caregiver in at-home hospice, and his terminal illness was nearing the end after a long and protracted struggle. Carys's father had been ill for a long time, but when his health began to deteriorate more rapidly, Carys, her husband, and her son moved into the guesthouse at her parents' property to take care of him. It meant that Carys had more time to spend each day looking after her father as well as helping her elderly mother with whatever else needed doing around the property, which was much appreciated—but of course, the inevitable downside was that she had less and less time to spend with her remaining horses.

Horses had become everything for Carys, and when she didn't have the time to be around them, her soul suffered noticeably. She missed everything about being around them, but what she missed most was their touch. For many years, Carys had been a massage therapist for horses, which meant that she typically spent several hours a day working on them in close contact. She used her hands, fingers, and elbows to massage their soft tissues, loosening their tight muscles, joints, tendons, scar tissue, and edema; increasing blood flow and lymphatic activity; and reducing stress. For Carys, it was not just a job, but a calling—a life mission. She had the privilege of spending hours every day with horses, helping them achieve better health, and she could think of nothing she would rather do. But with her father needing so much attention, she was required to cut valuable time from her schedule, and it was her horse time that was beginning to suffer. It wasn't an easy thing for Carys to do, but she knew she had to do something for the time being.

What Carys—and many of my clients—had discovered was that when you've been in the energy field of and touched an animal that much, you feel a closeness, a mystical connection that strikes at your heart when that animal's earthly life ends. It is an unshakeable bond, something that permeates your life in ways that those who haven't experienced it could never imagine. But as most people discover when they have lived their lives around animals, losing one or more of them is the price you pay for the love you shared with them. It certainly shouldn't mean that you don't want another.

And so, when the stray cat appeared, although she didn't realize it at first, it was a time when Carys needed a lot of comfort and joy in her life—a role the tiny kitten could fill to perfection. While to Carys, the timing may have felt like the worst possible for this needy stray to appear, in reality, it couldn't have been better.

Finn was a great example of that himself; he had been another stray who came to Carys at just the right moment in her life. Carys had found him at the intersection of a four-lane highway in Florida, and once she had taken the leap of faith and taken him in, he'd spent the rest of his life with her.

As with any animal, there had been an adjustment period while they each figured out their roles and what they needed to do to live together. Carys's husband, Ben, had built a cat door so Finn could come in and go out on his own. He had also learned to get along with Stormy, the family bird, a talkative African gray parrot known in the world of bird aficionados as the Einstein of the bird world. But Finn was smart, too, and soon he learned to stay away from Stormy's cage—anytime Finn got close, Stormy would kick food out of his cage, sending it down in a cascade on top of Finn, at which point Stormy would crack himself up in laughter. Fed up with repeatedly getting his coat sprinkled with birdseed, Finn soon learned to give Stormy's cage a wide berth.

As the end neared, Carys stroked Finn softly as he lay dozing in her lap every night, drifting in and out of sleep, in and out of consciousness. By then, he had wasted away to almost nothing, his coat thin, his whiskers ragged, his breathing barely a whisper. The thought of losing him soon was beyond overwhelming to her. How would she cope without him? Her father also had mere weeks to live. It felt as though circumstances were being piled upon Carys, pressing her into a state of sadness and depression that bordered on despair. She couldn't see a way out of it, and in some ways, she almost didn't want anyone or anything to try to provide one.

Then, into the midst of all that depressing sadness stumbled a scrawny black cat, whining under Carys's utility trailer with a desperate, hungry look on his face. He was still there—hadn't vanished overnight. Carys stood frozen, listening to the heartbreaking sound, peering into the shadows. Could she really ignore a kitty that needed her? He seemed so vulnerable and was clearly in need of help. She made her decision without even thinking about it. Despite her current situation, Carys fed him— her conscience left her no other choice.

As she walked back to her house, glancing back to see if the kitten had come out to eat the food, Carys told herself that it was a temporary arrangement, something short-term until she could locate a home for him. She stopped when she rounded the house, peering back around the corner—the kitten crept out, looked around, then devoured the food. Watching him, a warm glow surged in Carys's heart, and for the first time in what seemed forever, she allowed herself a smile.

However, during the days that followed, Carys had no luck finding a home for the stray. She kept on putting food out for the cat, and the cat kept eating it, but so far he remained timid and wouldn't come out when she was around. Clearly, he'd had some experiences that made him fear people.

Then, one night, the inevitable happened. Carys's elderly cat, Finn, passed away. That night, as Carys stood in the kitchen cooking dinner, the tears began streaming down her face at the loss of yet another beloved animal. Dinner was a somber affair, eaten in silence, with Carys's husband unable to provide any comfort. Then, just as they were clearing up the dishes, Ben called out to her. "Honey, look who just came through the cat door!"

Carys went to the living room to find the small black cat standing in the middle of the room, surveying his surroundings, his previous nervous disposition seemingly gone. Carys froze. She didn't want to spook him, wasn't sure what would happen next, and was, in fact, unsure what she wanted to happen. She needn't have worried. The cat seized the moment. After determining he was in a safe place, he trotted across the rug, jumped up on the couch, and began cleaning himself calmly.

Carys watched him for a moment, then scurried into the kitchen, returning shortly with a bowl of water and some food. The cat watched her carefully, then jumped down and sauntered over to the bowls. After devouring the food and drinking some water, he returned to the couch and settled down for the night. Within a few minutes, he was fast asleep.

Ben and Carys looked at each other and shrugged. "I guess we have a new cat," said Ben, chuckling. It immediately felt to Carys that this kitty had a purpose and that it somehow was meant to be with her. He had come to comfort her for all of the loss she had been experiencing and to ease her broken heart. And he, too, seemed to know what he was there for. He never acted nervous again and from that day on was comfortable around Carys and Ben, never showing any signs of his previous skittishness. They soon named him Dash, because he loved to run. He was a very independent cat and loved to roam outside, but whenever Carys called him, he would come bounding from who knows where just to be close to her.

While Dash loved to be close to Carys, he wasn't a cuddler and never wanted to be held. Carys was used to being very hands-on with her animals, but she respected Dash's desire for a little space and never tried to force him into any unwanted attention.

Dash had been with the family for just a few weeks when Carys's father's condition began to deteriorate more rapidly. He soon reached a point where he knew that his final hours were approaching. One evening, as Carys sat holding her father's hand and reading to him, Dash wandered into the room, peering up at them. Her father looked down, saw him, and smiled. "You know, I like that little fellow," he told Carys. "I'm sorry I won't get to know him; he seems very special."

Without thinking, Carys picked Dash up and placed him on her dad's chest. Rather than immediately jumping down and scampering away, as he normally would have done, Dash settled in, lying perfectly still and purring while her dad stroked his velvety fur. Carys's dad passed away soon after, but during his last few days, Carys often found Dash curled up on his chest while he slept.

After her father passed, Carys realized that she needed to change up the energy in her life to break out of her despair, and Dash seemed to sense what she needed. Although she wasn't trained in animal communication at the time, Carys had always had the ability to sense what animals were expressing.

Within six months of Dash joining the family, Carys had begun working toward getting certified in animal communication and energy healing. It felt easy and natural, with Dash by her side through each step of this exciting new chapter, encouraging her to step out of her comfort zone and be true to herself.

One evening, Carys was communicating with Chip, her son's three-month-old kitten, when she suddenly felt impelled to ask Chip, "What do *you* call Dash?"

She expected him to say *brother*, *friend*, or something to that effect, but she was surprised when Chip immediately replied, "I call him the wise one."

*Why the wise one?* wondered Carys. Again, Chip had an answer right away. He told her that Dash's roots went back to ancient times, that he had a knowledge that went back way before all of us, and that they could all learn from him. Carys had always known Dash was special, but Chip's message for her shared new insight into just how special. It gave her a much better understanding of Dash's depth and authority, an insight into why he had come to live with her. Part of his mission was to awaken Carys to a new and deeper level of connection. As a result of this and many other experiences with Dash, she is convinced that their partnership is not just happenstance, but divinely directed for a greater purpose—as it is with so many of the animals that choose us.

Dash loves his new role with Carys and now insists on being in the room for nearly all of Carys's communication sessions, lying close by, guiding her every step of the way. He helps keep her grounded, aids her in her connections with the session animals, and assists with the healing work. His specialty is bringing messages to others from beings in spirit, and Carys is thrilled that some of the messages Dash helps bring through are from her dad.

Since Dash came into her life, Carys has found that her understanding of her work has expanded greatly, as has her success, allowing her to focus much more on healing and communication. "He is most certainly an angel sent to help me on my journey of healing," Carys says. "I know we will always be together, and I am blessed that he is with me, guiding me to be a better me."

## Lesson

Animals often show up for us when we need them most—even when we may not know it at the time. Our meetings are divinely inspired and orchestrated more often than not. We may not know in the moment that an animal has entered our lives in the perfect season and the perfect way, but when we give them a chance and open our hearts and lives to them, it quickly becomes apparent. It can be helpful to look for and be open to these opportunities when an animal presents themselves in our lives. The love and connection they bring us just might appear when we need it most, and it can turn into our greatest gift.

As humans, we have a tendency to shut down when we are hurting, stressed, or traumatized. Unfortunately, this is rarely beneficial for us, as this is the time we most need to be open. When we're in fight-or-flight mode, it's difficult to be available for higher connections. If we can remain grounded, present, peaceful, and calm—which may seem impossible to do in the moment—we're much more able to notice the messengers in fur, sent to save us. Small things like noting your feet on the ground, breathing consciously, placing your hand on your heart—these may just be enough to give you pause and recenter yourself to a place of receptivity.

While Carys felt unable to help another being in need at the time, she didn't remain closed off, even though, initially, it seemed to be the most prudent thing for her in the moment. It turned out that the thing she thought would be a burden was the very thing that turned into a respite for her—and it has affected her life positively ever since. The help she offered the little kitty who showed up brought about his love and assistance in return and taught her great lessons. This is a wonderful example of the ways we can work to keep our hearts open to love and support, which can come in many different and unexpected ways. In doing so, we can develop a deep soul connection that will enrich our lives and usher us toward becoming exactly the person we were meant to be.

## Reflections

Reflect on a time when an animal showed up in your life at what felt like an inopportune moment but turned out to be in perfect divine timing.

1. Has an animal ever arrived in your life at exactly the right time to help you through something immense?
2. What helped you recognize this help and the timing of it?
3. Did this animal play a role in the transformation and expansion of your life?

## Exercise: Communicating with Animals in Spirit

When Dash arrived in Carys's life, he became the bridge and created the opportunity for her to learn animal communication, eventually with those in the spirit realm. Communicating with animals that are here on this plane and those that have crossed over is a very similar process, since we connect with them all at a soul level. I am a firm believer that the soul does not end with the ending of the physical body.

When your animal companions cross over, they are still very much available to connect with you from the spirit realm, just like they do on the physical plane. You may not be able to see, hear, or touch them the way you did when they were with you on this plane, but their love still surrounds you, and the connection you share with them is not broken, even by death. Some of the best ongoing gifts our animal companions offer us include the comfort and support they can give us from the afterlife.

Over the years, I've had thousands of connections with those in spirit form. If an animal friend has crossed over and you are looking for a connection or a sign from them that they are okay, an important step is to talk to them as you would if they were still here on this plane and ask for a sign. Then, wait and watch with heightened awareness for one to present itself. As I mentioned in chapter 16, if you're bogged down in grief from their loss, it can block your ability to notice their connections and signs, so be gentle with yourself, and allow yourself time to heal.

The following exercise can be done as a visualization or meditation—or, if you don't feel confident that you can do either of those options, simply go through the exercise and pretend or act as if you are doing it (you will still receive benefits from doing it this way).

1. Prepare a space as free from noise and distraction as possible where you can relax, undisturbed.
2. Uncross your arms and legs, straighten your back, and bring yourself into a relaxed and comfortable position—either sitting or lying down.
3. Take a couple of deep, cleansing breaths, inhaling through your nose and exhaling through your mouth. As you breathe in, visualize breathing in universal white light healing energy and exhaling any cares, worries, fears, or doubts you may have.

4. Visualize a beam of white light coming down from above and entering at your crown chakra. As it moves through your body, visualize it lighting up each of your seven chakras and exiting through your tailbone and the soles of your feet.

5. You are now connected above to Father Sky and below to Mother Earth.

6. Visualize your heart center fully open and receptive to the information your animal companion has to share with you (as you did in the previous exercises).

7. Tune in to your trust dial and visualize yourself reaching out with your arm and turning it up to high.

8. Now, clearly set your intention to communicate with an animal friend that has crossed over.

9. Call in your spirit animal and healing team to assist you with your communication.

10. Now, visualize Jiggs's Telepathic Pyramid extending from your third eye and heart chakras to your animal friend's heart chakra, forming a perfect pyramid for sending and receiving messages.

11. Take a moment now to intend that your channel is open to allow for clear passage of the information you will be sending to and receiving from the animal.

12. Call your animal companion's name three times out loud or in your head.

13. Ask your animal companion to come to you.

14. Ask them any question you'd like, perhaps about how they're doing or about their experience in the spirit realm. Any question goes here.

15. See what they have to share with you. Remember that their answer may be fleeting, and it may come to you in a form other than words.

16. Continue to share and ask anything you'd like of them.

17. Express gratitude for your connection and thank them for communicating with you.

I encourage you to revisit this exercise often to connect with animals in spirit.

## Chapter 18
# A Conduit for Healing

*Greatness does not come from trying to achieve the possible.*
~CONSTANCE FRIDAY

I worked for a number of years with a wonderful equine veterinarian named Sara. Sara had developed a great interest in my work, and she regularly shared with me her experiences as a vet. She loved expanding her knowledge on the wonderful ways that animals can communicate with us if we are open to them and was often surprised by how profound and detailed that communication can become when the circumstances are right.

Sara had participated in all my online training programs so she could learn my methods and be able to do this work for herself. Her journey had begun with her training in modern allopathic medicine, then over time, she had added traditional Chinese medicine and acupuncture as well as chiropractic to her tool kit, which had awakened within her a keen interest in other forms of holistic medicine. From there, it was an easy step to embrace energy healing and all the components of the spiritual realm. Sara was an avid and enthusiastic student and practitioner, continually devouring everything she could learn that might help her when she was working with animals.

In addition to her veterinary practice, Sara enjoyed doing liberty work with her own horses as well as teaching it to others on occasion. If you're unfamiliar, liberty work is a type of free-style horse training that requires no saddle or bit. The horse is set loose and the training is built on developing a sacred relationship between the horse and the person. You and the horse watch each other's moves and act accordingly so that you learn from each other, and thus, you develop an even deeper relationship.

Sara's was a busy life, which she relished. Equestrians generally have to be up early to oversee the feeding and care of their charges. As a bonus, Sara enjoyed being outside in the fresh air and sunshine, and then it was off for the day in her truck on farm calls.

In addition to the horses in her veterinary practice, Sara also consulted with me regularly for her own animals, whom she loved deeply. She not only had a collection of dogs, cats, and horses, but she also had various animals on the other side—in the spirit realm—with whom she was still spiritually connected and communicated regularly. Due to the scientific nature of their thinking and the type of training they have undergone, some veterinarians have a hard time mastering animal communication or believing in the power of energy healing. Sara, however, had embraced it fully and saw it as a vital part of her work, a highly valuable tool in her kit when she needed it. She didn't always tell her owners how she worked, but as long as the horses were healthy and happy, the arrangement worked for everyone.

As might be expected, Sara tended to develop deep relationships with all the horses she treated and cared for. This was especially true with her best friend's horse, Camarillo, a powerful and headstrong dark bay mare. Sarah did liberty work with her for several years, seeing her grow and flourish and developing such a strong bond with her that when her friend moved out of the country for work and couldn't take Camarillo with her, Sara gladly purchased her. She didn't mind adding one more horse to her brood, and she couldn't stand the thought of Camarillo having to start over in unfamiliar territory.

Sadly, not too long after Sara purchased her, she lost Camarillo to a quick and deadly illness that defied all treatment. After exhausting the possibilities, Sara spent Camarillo's final hour with her, stroking her mane and wishing with all her might that she could have done something more.

Sara was devastated by Camarillo's death, but rather than letting it discourage her, it spurred Sara on to learn even more about the horses under her care. Maybe there was something she had missed with Camarillo that might have helped treat her, Sara reasoned. If Sara could treat the animals better by furthering her training and deepening her understanding and communication with them, she would find a way to do it.

A few years later, Sara developed a similar deep relationship with another horse, Autumn—who, like Camarillo, was a beautiful bay mare. As it happened, Autumn was a gift from a dear friend, who was a horse lover as well and just knew the two would get along beautifully. The similarities between the two horses were huge and uncanny, and it was inevitable that Sara and Autumn would quickly form a powerful bond. After the pain of losing Camarillo, Sara had vowed to keep her emotions more in check, but somehow she just couldn't stop herself from falling deeply for this horse. Autumn was beautiful and had an irresistibly sweet personality to boot, and she took to liberty work naturally.

After several months of working with Autumn, Sara was proud of the progress they had made in liberty training. But one morning, to her utter dismay, something in the paddock spooked Autumn, who leaped, stumbled, and landed heavily on her side.

Sara never saw exactly what it was; she just raced to Autumn and could immediately tell she was seriously injured. Her brown eyes gazed up at Sara, betraying her pain, and Sara dropped to her knees and cradled Autumn's huge head in her lap. As Sara gazed down at her, whispering comforting words, there were tears in her eyes; she was hoping against hope that it was not as serious as it seemed.

Under Sara's supervision, Autumn was carefully moved to an equine hospital for a full range of diagnostics. The X-ray quickly revealed what Sara had feared—Autumn had sustained a very bad injury: a broken pelvis. Sara was heartbroken. Treating such an injury would be difficult at best, most likely requiring a long and arduous recovery period. And even if she did make it, Sara feared that Autumn would have no quality of life afterward. Her mobility would be limited, and she would probably be in constant pain. That was no life for any horse, particularly one as vibrant and energetic as Autumn.

Sara stared at the X-rays with tears in her eyes, forcing herself to focus, to view what she was seeing in a professional, dispassionate way, but the more she studied the images, the worse the injury looked. The images showed that not only were the ends of the bones two inches apart, they were also vertically displaced by over an inch. This was a major injury; there would be no happy ending for Autumn. The radiologist knew Sara well and knew how much she cared for her horses. "I'm sorry," he muttered as he peered over Sara's shoulder at the X-rays. Holding back her sobs, Sara mumbled a strangled "thanks" and stumbled from the hospital. Medically speaking, there seemed to be no hope for her sweet friend, and Sara couldn't justify keeping Autumn alive to be confined to a stall for her own benefit.

In my work with Sara, I had communicated with Autumn several times, and that very day Autumn called upon me and spoke to me very clearly, demanding that I call Sara and give her a message. To say that Sara was surprised to hear from me would be a huge understatement. "Lynn. This is unexpected," she said when she answered.

"Autumn connected with me and asked me to call," I told her.

"She did?" The past few days had been so full of shocks and surprises that Sara couldn't process or think of much to say.

"She insisted," I told her. Sara went silent, holding her breath. "Has she had some kind of accident?" I asked.

"Yes," Sara breathed. "She fell in the paddock and has a broken pelvis."

I tried not to react. That was a serious injury—no two ways about it. I got straight to the point. "Autumn understands her predicament but told me to tell you not to give up on her," I said. "She told me that she can heal from this. She also said that you can do it for her, Sara, that this is your time to shine, to step into your healing abilities in a brand-new way. You're not just capable, she told me, but a 'beyond brilliant' healer, with skills way beyond what veterinary school has taught you, even beyond what you can imagine."

"Oh my goodness," Sara uttered, choking up.

"Autumn believes in you, Sara," I concluded. "She said to trust yourself and your abilities as much as she does."

When our phone call finished, Sara wandered out into a paddock to think. Sara lay down on the thick grass and gazed up at the sky, trying to collect her thoughts. She knew what she wanted to do, but did it make sense? Was she brave enough to do it?

Then, suddenly, she smiled. Autumn had spoken, and she loved that horse with all her heart; how could she not try? My message from Autumn was not something that Sara could ignore, a sign from the universe that Sara was meant to do what Autumn had requested. Encouraged, Sara had no other choice but to find a way to help Autumn be healthy again.

While Sara's medical degree and training told her that what she was attempting was nearly impossible, having made her decision, she threw herself into the healing process with an open mind and a willing heart. She believed deeply in animal communication and trusted the connection I had with Autumn. It was a long road, but little by little, month by month, Autumn began to improve. Against all odds, Sara was able to heal her.

Before Sara knew it, Autumn was back to living an enjoyable horse life—not confined to a stall as Sara had feared, but free to enjoy life with other horses out in a lush pasture, which is any horse's dream. She had even returned slowly to the liberty work and was performing just as well as before.

Sara was beyond thrilled with Autumn's recovery. She'd used all her knowledge, allopathic and holistic, to heal her, even learning a new modality to help Autumn and enlisting the help of a fellow doctor friend who had further tricks up his sleeve. Her efforts had paid off, and Sara couldn't help but thank her lucky stars for Autumn's encouraging communication after the accident.

A couple of years later, Sara called me. "I think Autumn sent me a message and I'd like your input," she said tentatively. Sara had seen Autumn in a dream, and she had spoken to her. "She told me that there's a soul wanting to come into my life, and that she wants to be the vessel to make that happen. She wants to carry a baby, to deliver that soul to me in return for healing her."

I communicated with Autumn and she confirmed what Sara had said; in fact, she told me that she felt it was her mission to do this for Sara. After relaying my version of the communication,

Sara was ready to move forward. "Okay, then," she conceded. "We'll go ahead and find her a stallion."

Using the animal communication skills she had learned and practiced as well as her deep knowledge of bloodlines, Sara worked with Autumn to find the perfect sire. Autumn gave her input, and after poring over the choices and picking one they both agreed on, a baby was in the making.

Eleven months later, after having the best prenatal care a horse can receive, Autumn gave birth to a beautiful bay filly, whom Sara named Miracle—because she was one. Sara never thought the day would come or that the experience would be possible for Autumn.

Sara recognized an immediate familiarity in Miracle. She felt it strongly whenever she was around her, and especially when she looked into her eyes. Miracle seemed to feel it, too; she was instantaneously comfortable with and trusting of Sara, as if they already knew each other well. These feelings turned to thoughts of Camarillo that made Sara wonder if it could possibly be; she could barely believe it, but she suddenly felt with every fiber of her being that Miracle was the reincarnation of Camarillo. I confirmed it was true for Sara during a consultation—Miracle was the reincarnation of Sara's other love, Camarillo, the circle of life complete. Through their reuniting, all the loss and grieving Sara had held on to since Camarillo's sudden and untimely death fell away. Sara recognized Miracle as her miraculous gift, the culmination of Autumn's deepest mission—the one she showed Sara in the dream.

Sara now has her Miracle—literally and figuratively. Due to her openness to communication with her horses and her trust in her healing abilities, Sara was able to bring Autumn back from an almost certain demise and enable her to live a happy, healthy life.

And as an added bonus, Sara gets to do liberty work with both Autumn and Miracle at her farm, sometimes together—an absolute blessing for Sara and a just reward for her trust in herself and her love for Autumn. Having the spirit of Camarillo back in her life in the form of baby Miracle is a beyond-comprehension bonus. Against all the odds, Autumn's story did have a happy ending.

## Lesson

Many times, animals will surprise us with their knowledge, their tenacity, and their ability to heal themselves and others. Their intuition and gifts are still accessible to us even after they have crossed over, as long as we are open to and looking for the signs. When an animal is bonded with us at the soul level, the bond is unbreakable, even when they have crossed into the afterlife. The love we share with them does not cease to exist when they are no longer on our physical plane. It is important for us to remember that principle and to expect the unexpected.

In order to do the best she could do for her animal friends and become the highest and best version of herself, Sara had to step out of her comfort zone, take a leap of faith, and trust in herself and the messages from Autumn. It took tenacity and transcending the known, but her dedication to and deep love for her animal companions allowed her to focus on the outcome and do what she once thought was impossible. This is a strong testament to the fact that our minds are our only limitations, and when we are willing, we can accomplish more than we imagine with the help of our animal companions—and when you believe, miracles can happen!

# Reflections

Reflect on a time when you felt an animal companion was communicating information to you that you had to stretch yourself to trust.

1. Has your comfort zone ever been challenged by something you felt you needed to do for an animal companion?

2. What was being requested of you and what was the outcome?

3. How did heeding this information allow your brilliance and capabilities to expand and shine?

## Exercise: The Gift of Your Animal Companion

Simply by being with us over time, our animal companions bestow us with many gifts naturally through osmosis. They instill in us numerous positive qualities, including but not limited to the following: empowerment, transformation, inner peace, a greater sense of self, profound awareness, expanded creativity, a clearer vison of right livelihood, and the deepest sense of unconditional love many of us will ever encounter. They teach us and guide us toward new ways of being, motivating us to make significant changes in our lives—even the deepest ones imaginable— whether related to where we live, who we live with, or how we spend our time.

Our animal friends help heal us physically, emotionally, and mentally—and, in my experience, just by knowing them, our latent intuitive gifts begin to emerge, and we are automatically expanded into the highest versions of ourselves. Every interaction with our animal friends results in our expansion, even when it comes down to the often saddest time of all: their time to cross to the next dimension. It's been my observation during my career that even when our animal companions must leave their physical bodies, they leave us with a gift. Initially, in our grief, it may be hard to see or recognize that gift—or even conjure up any understanding of or positive thoughts about it—but upon deeper reflection, we can almost always uncover it.

Learning to understand and embody the lessons of the circle of life is one of the biggest and most obvious of the gifts their passing can offer us. We are forced to look deeper at the continuous and very natural cycle of life, death, and rebirth, which helps us understand the never-ending journey that all souls traverse and allows us to see—if we are willing—the continuing interconnectedness of all beings. Other examples of gifts we are left with are the knowing that we can always connect with the spirit of an animal friend and that they can bring us comfort, even once they have passed, and the understanding that our animal companion on the other side is continuing to assist us with life's day-to-day challenges. Even trusting that they're orchestrating the arrival of your next beloved animal companion is a gift.

I'm not saying that this doesn't take a leap of faith, a willingness to release the grief of their loss if they have passed, or a large dose of trust, but I am saying you will be all the richer for it if you can find a way to get there.

We're going to do a journaling exercise now to help you discover the gifts from your animal companion—whether crossed over or still here with you on the earth plane.

The following exercise can be done as a visualization or meditation—or, if you don't feel confident that you can do either of those options, simply go through the exercise and pretend or act as if you are doing it (you will still receive benefits from doing it this way).

1. Gather some paper, a journal, or some other means to record your experience.

2. Prepare a space as free from noise and distraction as possible where you can relax, undisturbed.

3. Uncross your arms and legs, straighten your back, and bring yourself into a relaxed and comfortable position—either sitting or lying down.

4. Take a couple of deep, cleansing breaths, inhaling through your nose and exhaling through your mouth. As you breathe in, visualize breathing in universal white light healing energy and exhaling any cares, worries, fears, or doubts you may have.

5. Visualize a beam of white light coming down from above and entering at your crown chakra. As it moves through your body, visualize it lighting up each of your seven chakras and exiting through your tailbone and the soles of your feet.

6. You are now connected above to Father Sky and below to Mother Earth.

7. Now, call forth an animal companion by name—one who has already crossed over or one who is still on the earth plane.

8. Take time now to reflect on your journey with your animal companion and the gifts they've instilled in you.

9. Begin journaling about them. As you allow your imagination to flow, be open to the information that comes forth.

10. Think of all that has transpired over the course of your time together and ask your animal friend some direct questions about it.

11. Write down any information or impressions that come to you.

12. Repeat steps 10 and 11 until you feel complete for this session.

13. Express gratitude for your time together and thank your animal friend for assisting you.

I encourage you to revisit this exercise to reconnect with your animal companion or to connect with another one.

# Chapter 19
# A Winged Ambassador

*Awakening is not changing who you are,*
*but discarding who you are not.*
~DEEPAK CHOPRA

This collection of stories would not be complete without the culmination of an idea that presented itself several times over, one that wove its existence throughout the book as smoothly and skillfully as a painter would add a sunset to a watercolor. In fact, it was not my original intent to include this element within the stories, but this particular animal persisted and would not be denied. Once I recognized the insistence and presence of these animals, I determined that it would be a disservice to not include them.

You may have picked up on the element of the red-tailed hawk occasionally throughout the book, and it is this majestic winged animal who kept making an appearance. In order to describe just how and where the red-tailed hawks have fit in, we must return to my story and the memory of my own animal companions.

After my precious golden retriever Jiggs crossed over on September 10, 2007, I got a Maltese puppy named Carly, as I mentioned briefly in chapter 16. She was an angelic, fairylike tiny ball of white fluff and the sweetest soul to ever live, and the two of us connected instantly. She was born October 19, 2007, just a short time after Jiggs crossed, although I didn't get her until the middle of January 2008. I had wanted to name her Chantilly Lace and call her either Tilly or Lacey. I was still deciding, so to determine what Carly's wishes were, I tuned in with her soul and asked her how she felt about the names I had chosen for her and whether she had a preference. She strongly related to me telepathically that her name was Carly, the name the rescue had assigned her for identification purposes, and she wanted to keep it.

A series of synchronicities was what brought me to Carly. Unbeknownst to me, the very night she was born, I arrived in Kanab, Utah, from British Columbia, where I lived at the time. I was getting ready to head to Arizona for the winter, but I wanted to spend a day at the wonderful Best Friends Animal Sanctuary first in honor of Jiggs. Sweet Carly wasn't even on my radar at the time, but imagine my surprise when I discovered that was the same night she was born! As I drove down toward Utah—and later again while driving from Flagstaff to Sedona—I received so many signs in the clouds from Jiggs that I knew were meant for only me to see. One as I neared Sedona was an amazing image of an angel, which I later knew to be my Carly, heavenly sent to me by him.

Carly, too, has since crossed over after being with me for over twelve years—her crossing occurred on the winter solstice of 2019 as I was working on this book. I miss her dearly, and as I mentioned, she came to visit me during the creation of this book as one of two red-tailed hawks riding the currents outside the sliding doors to my office, and she simply would not be ignored. She wanted my attention!

As a matter of fact, it was after this point that I realized more of these red-tailed hawks had decided they wanted to have their own place in the book, with hawk spirit stepping up and noodling its way in. Red-tailed hawks are commonly known as messenger birds, so when they show up, it's a good idea to take notice, as they will have a message to deliver! As I interviewed each client whose story is included within the book, I began to notice the hawks appearing in several of their stories. But it wasn't until the book was nearly completed that I finally decided to make the hawks an integral part of it. When Carly's spirit appeared to me in the hawk, it was as if I'd been hit over the head with the proverbial two-by-four! I'd been too engrossed in my work to notice the recurring thread that had been woven throughout the book all along. When I finally did take note, I knew the hawks needed to be included. Sheepishly, I admitted that in being so focused on the process of completing the book, I'd missed their many cues, and that it took them added effort to make me realize they wanted to be in it.

I have always found red-tailed hawks fascinating from both a physical and a spiritual point of view. The book *Animal Speak: The Spiritual & Magical Powers of Creatures Great and Small* by the late Ted Andrews has been a reference book for me for decades and is an excellent resource to learn about the significance of all animals. Much of the information I will share about hawks has come from it.

Hawks, especially the red-tailed variety, are "one of the most intriguing and mystical of the birds of prey," states Andrews.[8] They are powerful beings that are able to lead us toward our soul purposes, ushering us to higher levels of consciousness. With

---

8. Ted Andrews, *Animal Speak* (Woodbury, MN: Llewellyn, 1998), 152.

their sharp vision, hawks are known as visionaries of the air, having a keen sense of sight paralleled only by the owl. As visionaries, they have the capacity to help awaken a similar power in humans, guiding us toward awakening our inner vision and clairvoyance.

We can learn so many things from red-tailed hawks (as well as any animal, of course); their lessons and abilities cover a vast oasis of wisdom, and as receivers of that wisdom, we are truly blessed. One such lesson hawks teach is to "fly to great heights while keeping our feet on the ground." [9] I like to think of this as having roots and wings, which to me means that in order to best open to listening to and understanding animals, we need to be both grounded to the energy of Mother Earth as well as connected to the higher spiritual realms of Father Sky. For this reason, I have included exercises in this book to facilitate both connections, as I feel it's a crucial step to achieve the ongoing communion with the souls of animals—especially those who have already crossed over. As shown in the story of Jack in chapter 6, hawks can sometimes play an important role in assisting the soul of an animal (or human, even) by helping them cross over to the spirit realm. Think of them as guardians of the souls with the ability to bridge the gap between this world and the next. Hawks—but really, all birds—can also be vehicles for beings who have already crossed over to come back, connect with, and visit loved ones who are still on the earthly plane. Brightly colored and beautiful cardinals are especially known for this, so keep that in mind whenever you see the majestic bird or are looking to connect with a spirit being. When you see one flying nearby, pause, ground yourself, and open to any messages it has for you

---

9. Andrews, *Animal Speak*, 152.

to receive. Remember the steps of the exercises and see what you learn.

Another great lesson of the hawk is that they teach us to use our creative energies as well as our imaginations in unique ways. This can help us with our connection exercises, such as the visualization, meditation, journaling, and healing exercises in this book, as these are all creative pursuits, oftentimes requiring the use of our imaginations. It can also help with our animal communication and psychic abilities, as it takes creative energy to be able to listen to and fully receive the messages we are sent. In addition, it can take creative energy to interpret the messages properly, so cultivating that is important to the entire connection and communication process. It's important to keep in mind that messages we receive from hawks help us receive messages from other animals, too. Each interaction builds upon the other, growing us in knowledge and consciousness. There is always more to learn and room to grow.

I think at times birds can be easy to overlook in nature since they're all around us and we don't always take note. However, like all animals, they exist for a purpose—and even further, they are flying nearby for a reason! This is yet another example of the ways the universe speaks to us in the small things, but if we are too wrapped up in our busy rat-race lives; our own problems, projects, and hobbies; or our devices, gadgets, and screens, we may not notice. It's not always bad to be busy as long as we can remember to take the time to slow down and look around. After all, I'm not immune myself—look how long it took me to recognize the message of the hawks. Sometimes we're too close to the message to truly see it. Even after being in this field all these years, I'm still learning—the learning never ends. It's a lifelong process and a journey we should appreciate.

It is my hope that this red-tailed hawk thread inspires you to take your animal communication experiences a level further. It's great to start out with our companion animals and those close by, but next time you see a hawk—or any other animal in nature that catches your eye—stop and pay special attention. You just might receive a visit from the spirit realm or an important message, and you'll want to stay tuned.

## Lesson

Being open to and noticing the signs from animals, nature, our guides, and especially loved ones on the other side helps us deepen our awareness and greatly enhances our lives. When we allow ourselves to receive their messages, we are honoring them and the deep, loving bonds we share—even beyond the physical plane. Often, all it takes to do this is a belief that it's possible and a strong intention to receive their messages.

Just as the hawks with me, sometimes animal messengers are right in front of us—hiding in plain sight—and it takes them several tries to get through to us. Once we do recognize their presence and their message, it becomes clear that they were there all along. It can be easy to overlook them at times, though, which is why the animals often persist. It's also the reason to stop periodically throughout the day and ground yourself—quiet your mind and take a couple of deep breaths, allowing yourself to be open to and mindful of any messages being sent your way. In their deep love and care, our animals and guides desperately want us to receive and understand their messages.

All visitations from animal or spirit are especially meaningful, but particularly when we receive a visit from a loved one or animal friend who has crossed over. Taking the time to pause and assess the deeper meaning of their visit and message—whether via an appearance of a hawk, cardinal, or any other animal—can enrich our lives more than we might possibly imagine. It is my belief that once we've experienced messages from this higher plane, we won't want to go back because of the joy, fulfillment, and purpose we experience on a deep soul level.

## Reflections

Reflect on a time you've noticed an undomesticated animal showing up repeatedly in your life; perhaps it was a winged one, like a dragonfly, butterfly, cardinal, or hummingbird.

1. What animal was it?
2. Did you feel it had a significant message or meaning at the time?
3. As you reflect on it now, do you feel that it was a visitation from a deceased animal companion, or that it had any other significance?

## Exercise: Healing Portals Sent from Spirit

Our animal friends in spirit often visit us, just as my beloved Carly did in this story. Sometimes they offer love, comfort, and solace, and other times, they offer us divinely inspired knowledge, wisdom, guidance, and healing.

The knowledge and teaching they impart can even go as far as translating into an advanced healing technique. I mentioned in chapter 7 that Lucero, my Andalusian stallion guide—who was in spirit at the time—woke me up one night to offer me a download of a method of healing that he wanted me to learn and practice. I came to call it Lucero's Portal Points. It's been a very powerful tool to help release imbalances, blockages, and unbeneficial energies, and I've noticed that the animals I've worked with respond well to it.

**Lucero's Portal Points**

Using the information Lucero shared with me that night, we're going to do an exercise now on one of your animal companions to clear their energy field, provide healing, and possibly even receive messages from them during the process. Be sure to have some paper and a pen handy in case you wish to record your findings.

1. Prepare a space as free from noise and distraction as possible where you can relax, undisturbed.

2. Uncross your arms and legs, straighten your back, and bring yourself into a relaxed and comfortable position—either sitting or lying down.

3. Take a couple of deep, cleansing breaths, inhaling through your nose and exhaling through your mouth.

As you breathe in, visualize breathing in universal white light healing energy and exhaling any cares, worries, fears, or doubts you may have.

4. Now, visualize a beam of white light coming down from above, toward the top of your head (the location of your crown chakra). Visualize it entering there, slowly coming down through your body, and filling up every cell within you with this white light.

5. Then, visualize it exiting from the soles of your feet and the base of your tailbone.

6. Visualize it going down through the floor and any floors below you, connecting you and your energy deep within Mother Earth.

7. Now, bring your attention to your heart center (or heart chakra). Picture two small "French doors," roughly five to six inches in height, in the area of your heart chakra. These are doors that you can open at will.

8. Now, picture opening them outward in a way similar to opening the doors or windows in your home on a warm, sunny day. Experience the feeling of basking in the warm air and bright sunlight that come in, feeling great gratitude for this opening.

9. Consciously visualize and intend that your heart will be open to any information, in any form, that may come your way for the highest benefit of yourself, your animal companions, and all concerned.

10. Set a strong intention that simply by doing this exercise, your heart is now wide open and receptive to all information that comes your way.

11. Notice the way you feel in this moment—physically, emotionally, and mentally.

12. Choose an animal friend on this plane to work with.

13. Visualize your animal friend in front of you overlaid with a grid. Picture the grid like graph paper turned at a 45-degree angle, so that instead of squares, the pattern becomes diamonds. The diamonds on the grid overlaying your animal's image will most likely be larger in size than they are on a regular sheet of graph paper. Just allow the grid lines to appear naturally however they do.

14. Notice where the lines intersect.

15. Now, ask your animal friend to illuminate the inter- sections (or portals) with tiny lights (like fairy lights) wherever they would like you to clear or balance their energy.

16. We will work on these one by one.

17. Ask your animal friend to show you or highlight the "priority light" or "portal"—the one that your animal companion would like you to balance first.

18. Bring your attention to this light and focus your energy there, asking if there is any information about the imbalance they'd like to share with you. If so, make a mental note of it; if not, proceed to the next step.

19. Bring your attention to the priority light and mentally intend the deepest healing for your animal friend in that area on all levels—physical, emotional, mental, and spiritual.

20. Visualize a funnel of healing energy, swirling in a clockwise fashion and moving toward and entering the priority light or portal.

21. Visualize this light dimming until eventually it is gone as this healing energy permeates the area. Once the light is gone, that portal has been cleared and balanced.

22. Ask again if there is any information your animal friend would like to share with you.

23. Repeat steps 15 through 22 until you feel complete or ready to end the session—whichever comes first.

24. Be assured that you can come back to this often to help your animal companion clear further portals.

25. Thank your animal friend and feel gratitude for this process.

26. Feel your feet on the floor, take a couple of conscious breaths, and come back to present awareness.

27. Be sure to record the information you receive as you go or once you've completed the exercise.

I encourage you to revisit this exercise often to help heal and connect with your animal companion.

## Conclusion
# Activate Your Soul's Highest Calling

Powerful and transformational, the stories contained in this book have hopefully taken you on a journey, just as they did me. This book is merely a glimpse into the lessons and experiences I have been privileged to be part of since that initial moment Jiggs encouraged me to follow my calling.

Just as my own transformational journey began with Jiggs, it is my hope that you are either ready for or are well on your way to experiencing your own similar journey with an animal friend. By this point, you are aware of the transformational power and wisdom that is available to you through the animals, and I hope that the collection of stories I shared in this book is a catalyst for positive change in your life, whether big or small—because even the smallest change can have a far-reaching impact.

By assimilating the stories of others into your life through the written word and actively working through the reflections and exercises on your own, I hope that you are able to approach your life as well as your relationships with a different outlook than you had previously. I hope that through the information in this book, you find yourself open and awakened to the communication of animals as well as the healing gifts they have to offer you.

All the exercises contained in this book are designed to lead you toward your own experiences with animal communication and healing, and I promise you'll feel rewarded and fulfilled the more you give them a try. In fact, I encourage you to circle back and revisit the exercises until you feel you have mastered them; you will most likely find that you get even more out of them now that you've read the entire book. I urge you to go back and practice them until you become comfortable doing them and begin to see results, and then practice them some more! Ponder all the ways they relate to the stories, and then create your own story with your animal friend.

Each account in this book is a powerful reminder of some of the times animals have worked their magic in the lives of others. While these stories cover a wide range of experiences and show wonderful examples, that doesn't necessarily mean that each animal will fall into only one of those categories; many of them serve as multiple helpers for you or maybe even all of those mentioned throughout the book. There is no limit to the power an animal can have or what they can help us accomplish in our lives. The key is to remember to look for it, be open to it, and receive it with gratitude.

For me, being able to relive each of these familiar stories as I compile them into a book has been a renewing experience. Their power is as encouraging to me now as it was then, and I feel truly grateful to have been a part of all of them, and I am privileged to use my calling to help transform the lives of many others.

As I look back on my own journey, I can't help but think of how far I've come since that initial experience with Jiggs. I will forever be grateful to him for his guidance and everything he went through that led me to learn and find my true calling. I am also grateful to be able to communicate with him in spirit, and I appreciate his willingness to continue to help me, my clients, and my students from the spiritual realm. While I do miss him on this earthly plane, his presence is with me daily, as well as the other animals I've mentioned here and many I haven't.

Animal communicator, educator, and author Trisha McCagh has said, "Animals are the bridge between us and the beauty of all that is natural. They show us what's missing in our lives, and how to love ourselves more completely and unconditionally. They connect us back to who we are, and to the purpose of why we're here." [10] This quote is a beautiful reminder that both animals and humans are here for a divine purpose, and we can work synergistically to discover and join those purposes together for more powerful enlightenment and discovery. In doing so and in reaching expanded consciousness and further awareness, we are able to help others in their life journeys as well. Keeping in mind that animals are put here not to be simply pets but to be our companions, partners, teachers, guides, healers, catalysts, and bridges, we can approach them as the beings they are—important divine beings with deep wisdom to offer and help to give.

Each of us has a soul, and when our souls are awakened to all the possibilities at our disposal, we can work in tandem with other souls—both animal and human—to reach our highest purpose and calling. Thinking back on each person's real-life story in this book, you will notice that the transformation, guidance, and healing that happened in the lives of each of them only came to fruition when the person was ready and open to receiving them.

---

10. Trisha McCagh, *Stories from the Animal Whisperer* (New South Wales, Australia: Allen & Unwin, 2010), 11–12.

No matter where you are on your path, when you awaken to all that the animals have to share, you will be transformed beyond your greatest expectations. Are you ready to see where the journey takes you?

# Recommended Resources

Now that you are equipped with some of this information as well as the experiences documented within this book, you may want to go deeper on your journey and expand your knowledge further. I have two free resources for you that will help you get started.

1. My free Making the Heart Connection with Your Animal Companions training course will help you open even further to deeper connections with your animals as well as in every aspect of your life. It's a six-part audio series with a workbook and webinar. You can find it here: **https://lynnmckenzie.com/training/**.

2. My free Animal Communication & Healing Masterclass is a ninety-minute webinar that covers
   a. the three paths to animal communication mastery and how to know which is the best and easiest path for YOU;
   b. the number one skill you must master to expand your animal communication and feel 100 percent confident in your abilities;
   c. the key ingredient to understanding your animal companions confidently so you always know what they truly want; and

    d. the often-missed animal communication energy
    secret that instantly makes you feel closer to your
    animal companions.

You can find the class here:
**www.AnimalEnergyCertification.com.**

I also offer in-depth training programs and home study courses on a variety of topics to help you in the areas of animal communication and healing, psychic development, and clairvoyance mastery, which you can learn more about on my website, LynnMcKenzie.com. If you feel called to deepen your connection and explore a new path and calling, let me encourage you to take a deeper look.

## Connect With Me on Social Media

Like my **Animal Alchemy** Facebook page here: https://www.facebook.com/AnimalAlchemyLynnMcKenzie.

Follow me on Twitter here: https://twitter.com/animalenergy.

Subscribe to my YouTube channel here: https://www.youtube.com/user/AnimalEnergyHealing.

# Bibliography

Andrews, Ted. *Animal Speak: The Spiritual & Magical Powers of Creatures Great and Small*. Woodbury, MN: Llewellyn, 1998.

Coates, Margrit. *Hands-On Healing for Pets: The Animal Lover's Essential Guide to Using Healing Energy*. New York: Random House, 2012.

Dass, Ram. *Be Here Now*. San Cristobal, NM: Lama Foundation, 1971.

Junqueira, Heather, Thomas Quinn, Roger Biringer, Mohamed Hussein, Courtney Smeriglio, Luisa Barrueto, Jordan Finizio, and Michelle Huang. "Accuracy of Canine Scent Detection of Lung Cancer in Blood Serum." *The FASEB Journal* 33, no. S1 (2019): 635.10–635.10. https://doi.org/10.1096/fasebj.2019.33.1_supplement.635.10.

Maslow, Abraham H. *The Psychology of Science: A Reconnaissance*. The John Dewey Society Lectureship Series, no. 8. New York: Harper & Row, 1966.

McCagh, Trisha. *Stories from the Animal Whisperer: What Your Pet Is Thinking and Trying to Tell You*. New South Wales, Australia: Allen & Unwin, 2010.

Müller, Corsin A., Kira Schmitt, Anjuli L. A. Barber, and Ludwig Huber. "Dogs Can Discriminate Emotional Expressions of Human Faces." *Current Biology* 25, no. 5 (March 2, 2015): 601–5. https://doi.org/10.1016/j.cub.2014.12.055.

Nakamura, Kosuke, Ayaka Takimoto-Inose, and Toshikazu Hasegawa. "Cross-Modal Perception of Human Emotion in Domestic Horses ( Equus Caballus )." *Scientific Reports* 8, no. 1 (June 21, 2018): 8660. https://doi.org/10.1038/s41598-018 -26892-6.

Nawroth, Christian, Natalia Albuquerque, Carine Savalli, Marie-Sophie Single, and Alan G. McElligott. "Goats Prefer Positive Human Emotional Facial Expressions." *Royal Society Open Science* 5, no. 8 (n.d.): 180491. https://doi.org/10.1098 /rsos.180491.

Shakespeare, William. *Henry V.* The Bankside Acting Edition of Shakespeare. London: Gardner, 1910.

Smith, Amy Victoria, Leanne Proops, Kate Grounds, Jennifer Wathan, and Karen McComb. "Functionally Relevant Responses to Human Facial Expressions of Emotion in the Domestic Horse (Equus Caballus)." *Biology Letters* 12, no. 2 (February 29, 2016): 20150907. https://doi.org/10.1098/rsbl .2015.0907.

Stein, Diane. *Natural Remedy Book for Dogs and Cats.* 6th printing. Freedom, CA: Potter/Ten Speed/Harmony/Rodale, 2012.

## To Write to the Author

If you wish to contact the author or would like more information about this book, please write to the author in care of Llewellyn Worldwide Ltd. and we will forward your request. Both the author and the publisher appreciate hearing from you and learning of your enjoyment of this book and how it has helped you. Llewellyn Worldwide Ltd. cannot guarantee that every letter written to the author can be answered, but all will be forwarded. Please write to:

Lynn McKenzie
℅ Llewellyn Worldwide
2143 Wooddale Drive
Woodbury, MN 55125-2989

Please enclose a self-addressed stamped envelope for reply,
or $1.00 to cover costs. If outside the U.S.A., enclose
an international postal reply coupon.

Many of Llewellyn's authors have websites with additional information and resources. For more information, please visit our website at http://www.llewellyn.com.